TV
AS
ART:

Some Essays in Criticism

**Papers originally commissioned by
the Television Information Office
for the National Council of Teachers
of English Television Festival**

Edited by Patrick D. Hazard, Beaver College

NATIONAL COUNCIL OF TEACHERS OF ENGLISH
508 South Sixth Street   Champaign, Illinois 61820

TABLE OF CONTENTS

CONTRIBUTORS

PATRICK D. HAZARD

Department of English
Beaver College
Glenside, Pa., USA
Editor

JACK BEHAR

Department of Literature
University of California,
   San Diego

DAVID BOROFF

Formerly of New York
   University
Deceased

GEORGE BLUESTONE

Department of English
University of Washington

GEORGE DESSART

Executive Producer, WCBS-TV
New York, New York

RICHARD J. STONESIFER

Dean, College of Liberal Arts
Drew University

JOHN TEBBEL

Professor, Journalism
New York University

BROTHER THOMAS TIMOTHY, F.S.C.

Cathedral High School
Los Angeles, California

RAYMOND WILLIAMS

Fellow, Jesus College
Cambridge, England

CHARLES WINICK

Professor, Anthropology
   and Sociology
City College
City University of New York

MARIANN P. WINICK

Associate Professor, Education
Fairleigh Dickinson University

Patrick D. Hazard

TV As Art:
Some Reflections

The title of this collection appeared presumptuous to some who read the drafts of the book in mimeographed form at the 1964 Cleveland convention of the National Council of Teachers of English. These essays, in explication of significant TV programs, were commissioned by the Television Information Office for preliminary distribution at a Television Festival for English teachers organized by the former NCTE Committee on Commercial Broadcasting. Because many English teachers define their professional role as one of keeping clear the distinction between the aesthetically first-rate and the mediocre, they feel that TV in America has been so conspicuously "average" that it deserves the epithets non-art or anti-art or, at the very best, near-art. Accordingly, to talk about TV as art to a constituency of English teachers takes some explaining (which is not apologizing but may be mistaken for it).

One tradition which makes it difficult for the humanist to accept the possibility that TV programs can at least theoretically be "works of art" is the post-romantic defection of the refined aesthete from what he calls the pseudo-world of mass culture. He defines personal integrity and aesthetic quality by his distance from the predominantly shabby and jerry-built domain of industrialization. To him, TV is an example of the intrinsic shallowness of the mass-produced artifact.

Yet this facile theory of an aesthetic Apocalypse generates more and more doubt. Walter Ong, S.J., reminds us that the printed book was, after all, the archetype of mass production,

1

as indeed its appearance marked the beginning of mass communication. The simplistic division of human production into really fine and merely useful arts since the industrial revolution has proved ambiguous. Perhaps we need to remind ourselves that the original meaning of the word *art*, which is skill, makes the distinction. When men do a job well, they have worked artistically. Sometimes the action is individual, as in the creation of a lyric; sometimes it involves greater degrees of collaboration, as in the execution or completion of a fresco by a master's helpers; sometimes it is itself a paradigm of human society or the ultimate in collaboration, as in the construction of a Chartres. There is no metaphysical reason, therefore, why men working together in TV cannot create works of art.

That they rarely do is quite another matter. For men seldom achieve excellence in any medium. And the enfranchisement of the "untutored" masses in the cultural sphere has admittedly increased the percentage of the total aesthetic output which is mean-spirited and demeaning. This is as true of books (Mickey Spillane mysteries), of music (The Groaning Bones), and of movies (*How to Stuff a Wild Bikini*) as it is of television. So many more people have suddenly entered the cultural marketplace that the sheer volume of materials is overwhelming to the Arnoldian fighting an invasion with his few touchstones. Understandably, the emergence of a teenage culture designed to exploit the very immaturity a teacher is committed to exorcise has rattled us. It may be, too, that the prevalence of an "exploitative art" will be more than our schools can handle. Because America is the Land of Happy Endings, it is salutary for us to consider the possibility of failure. Some very respectable critics, Robert Brustein for one, have argued that the only defensible strategy for the humanist in mass culture is to teach his students to hate it. Trying to wheedle or cajole mass culture into maturity will only put the school at the mercy of commercialism.

This collection explores another possibility. If, to use Eliot's famous rationale, the critic's job is to put the reader in the fullest possible possession of the work of art, the TV critic's task is to make the viewer as aware as possible of what a TV program *is*. The method of explication, of showing how technique discovers meaning, ought to work on a significant TV work of art. It is reassuring to report that a critic like Cleanth Brooks finds such an assumption as obvious as it was to contributors to this experiment.

The cultivation of judgment about TV programs and other manifestations of cultural democracy must surely be one of the primary responsibilities of the contemporary school. Whether such cultivation best proceeds by a direct confrontation of mediocrity, a selective study of TV excellence, or indirectly from the study of literary classics is a pedagogical issue for which not enough evidence is available. This collection of essays makes it possible for teachers at every level of instruction, from elementary grades through college, to test the strategy of studying a few excellent works in the new medium.

Gifted teachers like Ned Hoopes at the Boston convention of the NCTE and thoughtful administrators like Henry Maloney in his editorship of "The Humanities Today" for *The Clearing House* have been suggesting the liberating potential of studying Socratically the "bad" programs our students watch *instead of* doing their homework. Imaginative teachers will want to try any and all of the approaches outlined, for example, in Neil Postman's *Television and the Teaching of English* (New York: Appleton-Century-Crofts, 1961). It is too early to know what the best ways are for raising the level of demand in the mass audience for better TV.

Granted that the English teacher accepts the challenge to raise the taste of the next TV generation, how does he keep informed about the new programs of merit before and after broadcasting? TIO prepares a monthly checklist of specials, *Scholastic Magazines* provides a weekly "Look and Listen" guide aimed at school needs, and local newspaper TV critics and TV stations can be persuaded to provide previews for teachers on an *ad hoc* basis. Most significantly of all for 1966-67,

NET's Henry Alter had a $.60 Guidebook prepared for the NET Playhouse season of forty weekly dramas. (Order from him, 10 Columbus Circle, New York 10019.) These are common sense approaches teachers and curriculum planners would be foolish not to use.

But, it seems to me, an alert English profession could take many more steps to insure that television fulfill its potential as a means of civilizing mass man. Let me first list the more important of these possibilities and then explore a few of them in some detail:

1. Provision that U.S. Office of Education curriculum centers and NDEA summer institutes take TV and other popular media into account.

2. Creation of an NCTE screening committee that would audit domestic and foreign TV and film, both commercial and educational, for programs ideally suited to English instruction.

3. Design of preview circuits to close the gap between the appearance of such materials and their use in curriculum.

4. Cultural exchange of television creators at the college level to encourage [our] best students to use their talents in the TV medium.

To spell out some of these opportunities, then, one properly begins with the federal government's generous funding of curriculum design and teacher retraining. There ought to be a small but irreducible place for outstanding TV programs in the work of the curriculum centers. It is inconceivable that forward-looking curricula ignore the newest medium. These new designs will influence the shape of curricula all over the country for the next generation. I should say that the inclusion of one program at every grade level for each element in the trivium—language, literature, and criticism—would be a way of insuring that TV not be ignored as it now is in the curriculum. Three works, carefully studied in the fashion suggested in the essays in this collection, is hardly too much to ask as a down payment on a gradually maturing medium. Similarly, one TV program bearing on each of the three components of the trivium would be a reasonable investment of time in the NDEA summer institutes.

The NCTE and the MLA might very well form such a screening committee as an outgrowth of two recent commitments. WGBH-TV, Boston, generously agreed to broadcast Robert Lowell's verse play based on Melville's novella *Benito Cereno* at the 1965 NCTE convention. National Educational Television made a kinescope of the one-hour-and-forty-minute play so that the Modern Language Association could show it to its members at the 1965 Chicago convention, when that organization began to alert its members formally about newer media materials. This program is an ideal test case. It is first-rate TV adapting a brilliant verse play by a major American poet working with a neglected nineteenth century classic. Novella, stage play, LP recording, TV program. Here is the raw material for real understanding of the complex media mix we must learn to live in and teach through. Because many English teachers are skeptical of audiovisualism in general and of TV in particular, we need a fresh opportunity to recover from our prejudices. NET has cleared the rights for this program so that it can be rented from its Audiovisual Center at Indiana University. From all reports, the first year of the institutes was not very successful at the media level. Here is a simple way to take a fresh start. A small committee composed of Melville specialists and media artists should be convened to prepare a repertory of materials about this TV program for the summer institutes. Out of their first very circumscribed task would develop more comprehensive ways of getting a few superlative TV programs into the literary curriculum.

In the course of preparing a report* for the U.S. Office of

---

* *Tradition and Innovation in the Craft of English: Reconnaissance for a War on Esthetic Poverty.* Copies available for $3.00 from Beaver College, Glenside, Pa., USA.

Education on using newer media in the teaching of English, I have had an opportunity to see what Canadian, British, and Irish television networks are doing for their schools. The teaching profession and the television industry in this country simply must devise ways of informing the schools of what is available from domestic and foreign networks. There is too much we don't know.

The simplest way to do this is to see that no professional meeting of any consequence goes on without its showing of new TV films. Local, regional, state and national convention committees should get in the habit of allocating "prime time" for one or two worthwhile examples of TV with teaching possibilities. Weekend workshops can also be built around the screening of such materials. ETV stations could telecast samples in their early Saturday off-hours (or right after school closes) so that an English department, for instance, could view films from commercial and educational TV which have recently gone into school distribution.

Finally, if we don't like what we see on TV, what can we do to encourage a new generation of creators to make television come closer to our first expectations for the medium? I think we have at this point the right, indeed the responsibility, to create a vision for TV. As we survive from day to day, playing Sisyphus to our mountains of themes, it would be a pity if we neglected altogether the humanities' responsibility to articulate an image and vision of a larger, better world. The anguish of transition will be too dear a price if a stable global community doesn't eventually emerge from the world's present painful chaos. The dream of a decent world community to follow the terrors and tensions of today's world is not a fatuous and unworthy hope when the only alternative is a nightmare of disaster. Television can play a major part in the efforts of good men to have humane values endure and prevail. And English teachers and professors, if they are not paralyzed by Eliot's version of a wasteland, can be crucial links in slowly building up the institutions of an international community.

In September 1965, the Commonwealth Broadcasting Union

met in Lagos, Nigeria, to plan ways for people in advanced countries to help design better communication systems in the less developed ones. In the same month, over a thousand artists from the same Commonwealth countries met in England for the first international Commonwealth Arts Festival. For the American English teacher, the coincidence of these two outgrowths of British idealism has an exciting implication: suddenly, all over the world, variants of English are being used to create new literatures in English. Nigeria has several outstanding novelists (view NET's "African Writers Today"). Ghana is filming its own interpretation of *Hamlet*. The BBC is producing excellent documentaries on the new "English" writers of the Caribbean, the Antipodes, the Asian subcontinent. The broadcasting services of these countries, hewing to the BBC tradition of respect for indigenous writers, are making at least part of a world community a reality.

We need to inform ourselves about these new revealers of our expanding subject matter, English. We need to bring from these various emerging nations writers to be in residence here, and we need to send our best creators abroad so that TV may become a major link in the communication chain that precedes a humane world order. My experience viewing this world television in Toronto, Dublin, London, Geneva, and Paris convinces me that English teachers would not only be exhilarated by the first artistic evidences of a global civilization, but they would also want to share in creating more English-speaking television as one medium of a slowly crystallizing world society full of marvels. Indeed, the first task of a world association of English teachers, I think, should be a gathering of the best TV being created throughout the English-speaking world.

American commercial television has a firm commitment to world TV. It could perform a service to our profession and to our collective desire for a world safe for diversity if it underwrote annual chrestomathies of world TV in English, beginning at the 1966 NCTE convention in Houston, the Space Capital of the world, and at the 1967 one in Honolulu, whose East-West Center symbolizes our desire to live with our Asian neighbors in mutual respect. I suspect commercial TV might even, in the process, find some programing they would want to include in their own schedules. They would have the continuing gratitude of an English profession appreciative of a volume of essays like *TV as Art: Some Essays in Criticism.*

John Tebbel

The Making of a President: Politics and Mass Communication in America

Few documentary films in our times have come as close to the meaning of America as *The Making of a President*, based on Theodore White's best-selling account of John Fitzgerald Kennedy's progress from the primaries to the White House. If the book was a masterpiece of the journalist's art, the television film derived from it and presented on the ABC network had that literary, poetic quality which one remembers from *The Plough That Broke the Plains*, *The River*, and in still photography, the superb Farm Security Administration portraits of America and Americans during the depression.

It was not so much Martin Gabel's smooth narration of White's script nor the words of the candidates themselves which made this so. Rather it was the succession of vivid images depicting the people of the United States engaged in the most mysterious process of this democracy, the election of a national leader. In the phrase of the avant-garde, it was a triumph for *cinema verité*.

In its construction, *The Making of a President* is in effect a story which begins with a large landscape on which there are many figures, with the focus gradually narrowing down until in the end there is only the closeup of a suddenly lonely man separated from his fellows by the high responsibility they have given him. In another sense, it is like a ballet in which the politicians follow a long established choreography—a ceremonial, ritual dance, in which the patterns are scrupulously observed.

On the initial broad canvas, the characters move in established modes. We are shown first Mr. Kennedy, Hubert Humphrey, Stuart Symington, Lyndon Johnson, Adlai Stevenson, Richard Nixon, Nelson Rockefeller, and Barry Goldwater, denying in various ways that they want to be President. Then the positions change, and we see the same people earnestly seeking to test their potential strength in the primaries, obviously with their minds on the White House, as they have been from the beginning.

Images of America flood the screen as the hectic days of the primaries are recorded, and in some respects these are the most significant portions of the film. They depict with a startling clarity the extremes of our culture and, in a more subtle aspect, the strange position which the political man occupies in that culture—at once a backslapping, baby-kissing, handshaking part of it, and at the same time a withdrawn, alienated figure because he has set himself off from his fellows by presuming to represent them. The shadow of the White House falls on the lesser figures as well.

Two shots make these points in a particularly vivid way. One is the view of an entire hamlet's population in New England sitting around a rude table and casting its primary ballots. Rural America is disappearing, the film seems to be saying, but we are not yet separated from our past; and the workings of our political system, past and present, are brought into silent, unacknowledged conflict, with implications which apparently no one but philosophers have the courage to consider.

The other shot is especially striking, with the advantage of hindsight. Mr. Kennedy is on a handshaking tour, as are his rivals, and we see him early in the morning outside a factory. Some of the men stop to shake his hand, others glance curiously and go on, many ignore him, and he stands athwart the stream of going-to-work laborers looking somehow out of place, almost pathetic as the crowd flows by. Yet we know that in a few short months he will be the object of nearly every American's absorbed attention, surrounded by the authority and power of the Presidency. Few shots in the film make this point more effectively, yet it is done entirely by indirection.

These and other views of the primary campaign also delineate the essentially small-town character of America—crowds in the street, around the courthouse, lifting faces in which politicians can read nothing for certain until the ballots are counted. They are comfortable, middle class faces for the most part, friendly but reserved, interested but uncommitted, and the camera looks down upon them as the candidate sees them. The perceptive viewer, identifying himself with that candidate, can feel only sympathy for the man trying to reach behind those faces to the prejudices, convictions, passions, bigotries, opinions, and personal moralities lying inside.

After viewing the electorate in sequences which move rapidly about the country in the key primary states, the contrast is again vivid and effective as the focus narrows for the first time and we move onto the relatively restricted stage of the nominating conventions. Here is the ritual dance once more, but the editing is brilliantly done in showing us the real mainsprings of the performance—the carefully planned and timed Stevenson demonstrations, the lights burning late in Mr. Kennedy's hotel hideaway, the conferences of behind-the-scenes maneuverers, all in sharp contrast to the windy, dreary hoopla of the convention floor.

The focus narrows once more. Competitors fall away in the rollcalls until only Mr. Kennedy and Mr. Nixon remain. They emerge abruptly as the two protagonists of a mighty drama— the campaign to elect a President. With the advantage of retrospect, we observe the temporary eclipse of Goldwater and Rockefeller, knowing as we do what resolves were then taking place in the minds of Senator and Governor.

In Lyndon Johnson, we are shown another aspect—the politician who accepts and waits his time, satisfied for the moment to be a member of the supporting cast, an honorary second best. Earlier there is a memorable primary campaign scene in which Mr. Kennedy and Mr. Johnson, fighting hard, even desperately, for the nomination, appear on the same platform and fence

jovially with the heavyhanded humor of fellow club members.
(Lyndon Johnson tells the crowd how hard he has worked
night and day in the Senate, boasts of what he has accomplished, and sits down. John Kennedy agrees with everything
he says and advises the audience not to lose a splendid Senate
majority leader by making him President.)

Now follows the most dramatic portion of the film, in which
action and sound blend in a rising crescendo. Here we begin
to sense the fateful and perhaps decisive role television played
in the campaign, not only in the debate between the candidates, but implicitly in the way Mr. Kennedy adapted easily to
the medium as compared with Nixon's obvious distaste for it.
This point is adroitly underlined in the shots of the debates,
where the camera, from a vantage point in the television studio, records the words and actions of the two candidates before they go on the air. There is Nixon, first on the scene, appearing not to understand clearly what the director is telling
him, looking tense and preoccupied. Then Mr. Kennedy arrives
late, the picture of calm confidence, taking the studio situation
quickly and firmly in his stride. As the candidates begin their
debate, the narration points out how Nixon adopts the stance
of the college debater, addressing himself to his opponent, while
Mr. Kennedy speaks directly to the cameras and the millions
beyond them, hardly appearing to notice Nixon.

As the campaign moves to its climax, with the camera following the candidates from city to city, the sound track rises to
a peak of intensity so that the abrupt switch to election day becomes a dramatic piece of editing. Suddenly it is quiet. The
voices of candidates and crowds, which have mounted higher
and higher from the beginning of the film, end as though cut
off by a knife. It is the morning of election day, and we see the
voters going quietly to the polls, standing in line, filing soberly
into the voting booths. The fate of the country is in their hands
now, and somehow the impact of this truism strikes even the
sophisticated viewer with a force he might not have believed
possible.

There is a brief, tense interlude while the votes are counted and the candidates wait, alternately hoping and despairing as the fluctuating returns place Mr. Kennedy, then Mr. Nixon, in the lead. The candidates and those closest to them wait anxiously. A still photo of the Kennedy entourage, viewed in harsh black-and-white light, catches the frozen suspense of those moments. Then, as it seems that Mr. Kennedy will win, the film makes one of its most telling points by cutting to another watcher of the returns, the director of the Secret Service, who rises from his comfortable living room chair, in itself a symbol of the ordinary citizen's privacy, to make the telephone call which will set in motion the machinery of protection and send security agents filtering quietly into and around the Kennedy compound at Hyannisport. For John F. Kennedy, privacy is ended with that act. Now he belongs to the whole country.

Seen as a whole, *The Making of a President* puts the viewer somewhat in the position of the Secret Service director. In his own living room chair, the citizen shares vicariously with the candidates in the democratic process. He is a part of it, exercising his ballot as the director exercises his special authority, yet he is separate.

The viewer knows about power, reads about it, talks about it, but in this vicarious experience through his television screen he gets a concentrated impression of how it feels. For White's book and the film itself are essentially about power. Its insights, furthermore, relate power to the life of the average citizen. Looking at the capsule biographies of the candidates—their birthplaces, class pictures, athletic teams, small beginnings— he can sense something of the mysterious process which translates a Stuart Symington from Missouri, an Adlai Stevenson from Illinois, a Lyndon Johnson from Texas, and so on. If there are other factors involved which may have given one man a privileged start over the other, the average viewer is not likely to be concerned about it. What he sees is that these people are Americans too, rising out of obscurity like his own, from small frame houses and little towns like the ones he has known. Sometimes this particular insight meets an insuperable obstacle like Nelson Rockefeller, but then the Rockefellers are accepted for what they are, and after all, didn't the founder start from nothing, like everyone else?

Another familiar quality which enables the viewer to identify with what he sees is the portrayal of politics as a game. Its clichés, its maneuvers, its special vocabulary are well known to everyone who watches. Consequently when the film cleverly gives us a sequence of quotations from the candidates before they become candidates, in which they solemnly aver that it is much too early to make a declaration, or even deny that they intend to make one, the viewer smiles knowingly. He has heard it all before. The candidates are making the expected responses at the proper time, and it is as familiar to the American citizen as any game he happens to fancy. It is ritual, dear to the hearts of Americans. As perennial joiners, whose fabric of social life is bound up in thousands of organizations, most of them ritualistic in some way, they want politics to follow the established order too, because they feel at home with it.

As he watches the candidates campaign, the viewer must also get a sense of how much the same, yet how different he is from his fellows in various parts of the country. Those faces watching Kennedy plod through the snow of New Hampshire are New England faces, but they have a close kinship with those other faces at the factory gates in the Midwest or in the prairie country. The environments are so different, the regional backgrounds are different, yet the watching citizen cannot help being conscious of his common heritage with other Americans, and perhaps appreciating, without consciously thinking of it, what it means to be united in a single government.

Something of these differences is implicit in the approach of the candidates to the voters, and here the emotions of the viewer can become mixed indeed. As he watches Hubert Humphrey's warm, friendly mingling with the voters, his old-shoe approach, as compared with the cool, calm efficiency and the New England restraint of Kennedy, he may wonder in retrospect what it was that made this rich man's son with an accent strange to most Americans outside his region prevail against the folksy image Humphrey was projecting. Perhaps he will

understand something of the answer as the film unfolds and he
sees the candidates in action. There is, for example, the raw
courage of Kennedy appealing to the best instincts of the Bap-
tist ministers in Texas. Indeed, his fight against bigotry is underlined several times in the film, appealing to the American
sense of fairness. Again, there is Kennedy in West Virginia,
which should be alien to him and his religion, but in the faces
of the primary campaign crowds there is respect, not hatred.

This is not to say that Humphrey is depicted unsympatheti-
cally, nor is any other candidate. The producers have been
scrupulously fair in their editing, and the point is made as
Humphrey withdraws from the race that he leaves behind him
a glow of devotion. Nevertheless he withdraws, and the viewer
understands it better when he sees the authority and confidence, the intimation of greatness, which emanates from Kennedy everywhere he goes. It is something that must be seen to
be understood.

In the convention scenes, the viewer is given another aspect
of the Presidency ritual which he may not find so reassuring if
he thinks about it. Just as emotional fervor does not get Humphrey nominated, neither does it get the party nomination for
Stevenson, in spite of his dedicated, wildly zealous followers.
The film makes this point by contrasting the floor demonstration for Stevenson with scenes in the Kennedy suite, where the
candidate's entourage is confident, serene—and organized. The
smiling, civilized face of Stevenson, the political Hamlet, is a
sharp contrast to the sheer youth of the Kennedy image as it is
projected from the screen. Kennedy smiles too, and it is a
warm, endearing smile, but it is controlled, and when he listens
to the other candidates on the same platform his is the only
face which is cold and abstract and makes no pretense at the
polite smiling interest which the others show.

The television camera is merciless in conveying subtleties of
character, and they are observed in even sharper focus in this
film which brings them together cheek-by-jowl over an intensely concentrated stretch of time. The viewer will not be
likely to forget, once he has seen it, the blandly calculating

faces of Nixon and Rockefeller after their historic meeting in New York, nor the outraged look of Goldwater in Chicago declaring to his fellow Republicans, "It's a surrender to Rockefeller."

But perhaps the most important point the film makes in this respect is the contrast between candidate Nixon on television in the great debate and the Nixon who speaks from the rear platform of the campaign train. Nowhere is the profound influence of television more obvious, even to the untrained eye. Nixon is at his best when he is alone with a partisan crowd; in direct competition, as one of his managers remarked after the campaign, he obviously has a glass jaw.

Near the close of the film, another subtle point is made which comes close to the meaning of the whole thing, and again it is something the viewer can understand. The returns are in, Kennedy is elected—and suddenly those around him who have been so close to him for months on such intimate terms greet him with a certain shyness. He is not one of them anymore. He is the President of the United States.

Television has made us familiar with the sight and sound of Presidential inaugurations, but at its close *The Making of a President*, in showing the figure of the new Chief Executive taking the oath of office, must have made a great many viewers understand as they never had previously what it means to be one man among many and then, within a few months, to be the single representative of all.

Viewed as a whole, this television film must be considered as one of the best efforts yet made by the medium. Without rhetoric or "preaching," it tells Americans what their country is about, displaying it in both its formidable strengths and its lamentable weaknesses. Like a great novel, the film moves on different levels of meaning. In one sense it is sheer choreography, a ballet with an unusually long *pas de deux*, moving smoothly from ensemble to solo. In another way, it is a commentary on the democratic process, reducing the mystique of the American political experience to its most practical application. In a reverse sense it conveys that mystique—the sense of tradition, of inevitability—in the most memorable terms. No viewer with a feeling for history can watch this film without feeling that he is part of an awesome historic process in which the figures of the mortals who move on the stage are at once pygmies and ten feet tall.

By translating and synthesizing the great American political experience, *The Making of a President* well serves the educational function of television for which so much was hoped at the beginning and which has been so little fulfilled. It also illustrates, in various ways, how large a part television has come to play in American political discourse.

The dimensions and meaning of that role have become one of the continuing debates of our time. We accept the primary proposition readily enough—the self-evident fact that television has changed political life in the United States by exposing the candidate to the electorate with the uncompromising clarity of the camera eye. As a corollary, we also accept the manner in which the Presidency itself, politically speaking, has become in essence a public relations problem because of the influence of the mass media, particularly television. But we are not quite so ready to embrace some of the consequences which flow inevitably from these facts.

Now and again there rises a chorus of complaint from those who observe Lyndon Johnson, the master in using public relations as a Presidential tool, as he goes about manipulating television in much the way he does individuals. Some of this complaint is purely political, true enough. It is naturally galling for Republicans to see a Democratic President spreading his image far and wide, and selling his views as skillfully as though he were a salesman making house-to-house calls.

But there is another aspect of this matter which was well illustrated by the Dominican crisis in the spring of 1965. In those confusing days, when the President's action was being hotly debated even while it was taking place, Mr. Johnson used his power as President virtually to commandeer television as a platform for defending and justifying his actions in the Dominican Republic. That gave him a tremendous advantage over his critics, who could not command the instant audience that a Presidential broadcast gathers.

It was not an altogether successful effort, however. The President overdid it by appearing too often. The networks could not, or did not, clear time for him in concert; sometimes he was taped and rerun at a more convenient (for the broadcaster) time. His ratings also declined with the frequency of his appearances. There were complaints that he was crying "Wolf!" too often, and sometimes without sufficient reason. In the end, Mr. Johnson suddenly disappeared from the screen and was not seen for some time.

But the incident was instructive and sobering in demonstrating the potential power of a President, using a medium which can reach fifty million people or more at once, to imprint his personality and his views on the consciousness of a nation. Anyone who read disturbing 1984 implications into that ability could be consoled by the fact that in America, at least, a President who appears frequently and at moments which are not necessarily historic or critical places himself in competition with other shows, designed for entertainment. In this competition, much as the intellectual community may deplore it, entertainment always wins hands down. Presidents not only suffer from overexposure, as some show business figures do, but in a sense they have to entertain an audience as well as inform it. Lyndon Johnson giving an historic civil rights speech to a night session of Congress is not the same as Lyndon Johnson taking fifteen minutes of time to defend himself from his political critics, particularly if the fifteen minutes is subtracted from a commercial program with a high rating.

Nevertheless the astute use of television adds another dimension to the Presidency, just as radio did with Franklin Roosevelt's "fireside chats," which so enraged Republicans in exactly the same way Mr. Johnson's communings with the voters do now. In the hands of a President who understands the manipulative techniques of public relations, as Mr. Johnson does and as Mr. Kennedy did, television can be a formidable political weapon, and there is no question that it will become more so as time goes on.

To turn to another aspect, we might ask ourselves what the far-reaching effect may be on the political process of the requirements now imposed on political candidates that they must be photogenic to be successful. In the discussion which followed the television debates between Mr. Kennedy and Mr. Nixon, much was made of the contrast between the Bostonian's distinctive Irish good looks and boyish charm, and the jowly Nixon countenance with its heavy beard stubble which showed darkly on the television screen. There were some commentators who believed that the election pivoted on that television contrast—the buoyant, boylike Kennedy and the gaunt, obviously weary, stubbly Nixon. Incredible as it seems in retrospect, there were disgruntled Republicans who blamed the television makeup man for not exercising his art more successfully on the candidate. It was even said, only half-facetiously, that he might have been a Democratic plant.

Did the election really depend on the television image projected to the electorate by the two candidates? The sophisticated political analysts scoff at the idea, and they point to a combination of other factors—traditional and ascertainable matters like shifts in the Negro and labor vote. Yet it is noteworthy that President Johnson, the most consummate politician since Franklin D. Roosevelt, gave so much weight to the possibility that he skillfully maneuvered himself out of facing Senator Goldwater in a proposed renewal of the television debates during the campaign of 1964.

The President knew that he showed to better advantage in face-to-face meetings with the voters. In any case, the White House had already acquired television's point of view, and the danger of overexposure was taken into consideration. The nation sees a great deal of its President on television as it is, and undeniably there is more authority in such appearances by the Chief Executive than as one of two debaters.

The truth is that no one can be certain of the full effect of television's pitiless portrayal of people. The debates may have been an important contributing factor to Nixon's defeat in 1960, but it is possible that the ill-advised "Checkers" broadcast of 1952 was a root cause. Did this folksy, bathetic interlude have an opposite effect than the one intended and leave viewers with a subtle distrust of Nixon which the later debates only emphasized? No one knows for certain, but it is safe to say that television was a primary factor in stopping Nixon's career short of the White House.

In the short time since David Sarnoff brought television officially upon the public stage with the opening of the World's Fair in 1939, the medium has given us the vibrant image of Roosevelt, hardly dimmed by his illness; the sincerity and integrity of the Truman image, which was enough to triumph over the polltakers and the professional politicians; the overwhelming photogeneity of General Eisenhower, which combined with the hero-as-politician image to defeat Adlai Stevenson, whose intellectualism was so well conveyed by television that it dismayed the rank-and-file; and finally, the image of youth triumphant in Mr. Kennedy.

One need only look back briefly into history to comprehend how much television has altered the face of politics. Would the greatness of Lincoln have been enough to override his high voice and backwoods appearance if television had projected him to the whole electorate? One might ask the same question of George Washington, whose Virginia voice was also rather high and, conceivably, with its soft southern accent might have been irritating to the militant Yankees of the Northeast, where most of the votes happened to be. At a later time, one cannot help wondering how history might have been altered if Woodrow Wilson had been able to carry his plea for the League of Nations to the entire nation by means of television rather than waste his declining strength on a futile road trip. Could Calvin Coolidge have been elected if television had disclosed his utterly colorless personality in direct contrast to the lively image of James M. Cox?

We cannot change the past, but there is every indication that television will profoundly alter the future of political dialogue in America. It has, for instance, already given the Presidency a formidable weapon which one may be certain no President will hesitate to use. There was a first hint of this kind of mass media influence in F.D.R.'s "fireside chats," on radio, and when the Roosevelt magic was later transferred to television, portents of the future sent a premonitory chill down the spines of men in both parties. We have witnessed since then the steady growth of the televised press conference and observed how effectively it could be used in the hands of a master like Kennedy and how revealing it could be in the less eloquent hands of an Eisenhower. Since Mr. Kennedy's death, we have had another lesson in the constant, varied use of television by Mr. Johnson, who has a great politician's sure instinct for using the mass media.

The most striking demonstration of television's power in politics was its role in bringing down Senator Joseph McCarthy where everything else had failed. The demagogue who defied the President himself and seemed to loom larger than the United States government, certainly the most frightening figure in American politics since Huey Long, was marked for destruction by the medium he obviously believed would only increase his power. When the Army-McCarthy hearings brought him into everyone's home instead of only within the ken of frightened public men and intimidated private citizens, the wave of public revulsion washed him into oblivion.

Again, one cannot help speculating about two possibilities. Suppose there had been no television to check and destroy McCarthy? In the beginning it had been feared that television would help demagogues to power; now it appeared that they could be unhorsed more easily than they were made. The McCarthy affair demonstrated that television could make the national will more responsive to political situations than it had ever been before.

The other speculation is historical. If television was able to dethrone McCarthy, what might it not have done to change the course of history by eliminating other rogues, which leads to the further thought that it might well be the means of improv-

ing the morality of politics in America. That politicians are
aware of this potentiality is evident in their determined resistance to the televising of legislative proceedings except under
carefully controlled conditions, or for self-serving purposes.
Always cited is the danger that some politicians might use television as a public platform, but the danger is exceeded by that
of having the voter's eye upon the legislator as he legislates.
There would be, perhaps, no shorter route to drastic reform.

There is a good reason, however, why the politicians have
nothing immediate to fear. As television's news function has
expanded and the art of electronic journalism has developed, it
has edged more and more into the areas once the exclusive
property of newspapers. But even though the nature of the
medium gives it a decided advantage in the coverage of on-
the-spot news, it does not possess the freedom guaranteed to
newspapers by the First Amendment and, in fact, is edito-
rially under the heavy hand of Congress, although normally
it is regulated by the Federal Communications Commission.

Frequently the FCC urges broadcasters to editorialize more,
to exercise the democratic privilege of free comment on the
news it covers. Many stations have taken the Commission at its
word. They have not only editorialized but have gone much
further than endorsing the Boy Scouts or urging the commemo-
ration of Arbor Day. A few have become persuasive editorial
voices within their communities, but others have encountered
head-on the drastic limiting factor which potentially threatens
every station. These unfortunates have had the courage to attack Congressmen or Senators from their own districts, and
those attacked have written none too subtle letters to the FCC
demanding that the activities of the offending stations be in-
vestigated before their licenses are renewed. This is the club
that members of Congress hold over television and radio. The
FCC is the creature of Congress, dependent for funds and existence on its will. While no one imagines that Congress would
dare end the life of the FCC for political reasons, or for that
matter would ever want to do so, nevertheless the FCC is extremely sensitive to Congress, and the fate of individual sta-

tions under its jurisdiction is another matter. Pressure and the fear of pressure are always present in the local station. The courageous defy it. The others simply censor themselves and say nothing.

For these and other reasons television can never play quite the same role in the national political dialogue that newspapers have done. The role it does play, however, may be much more significant. In terms of the Presidency, it could conceivably create a cult of personality of a kind deplored by the post-Stalinists, and indeed it has made some long steps in that direction. Moreover, it can be used effectively, in company with other media, as President Johnson has demonstrated, as a public relations device to create the most favorable possible image of the man in the White House.

What is that image? Increasingly, it has been the actor-hero— a photogenic personality who projects himself larger than life. It was said during the Dewey campaign that William Howard Taft was the last man with a mustache who could have been elected President, but it may be equally true that Calvin Coolidge and Herbert Hoover were the last quiet, reticent, unheroic figures to reach the White House.

Aside from the Presidency, television has performed a public service in airing controversy (to a somewhat limited extent, however) and in exposing politicians to a national audience. A Senator who appears on *Meet the Press* is exposed to more than his constituency. If he aspires to nothing more than re-election, and if he comes from a state where he is entrenched, it will not matter how the national audience regards him, but if he has larger ambitions, the television appearance becomes a critical episode in his career.

Programs like *Meet the Press* perform another useful function in providing a forum for the discussion of ideas in the continuing dialogue between electors and elected. Their usefulness, however, is limited by the skill of the interviewers in prodding the guests out of their platitudes. The moments of revelation, when they come, are likely to be significant enough to carry over into the daily press, thus enlarging the audience of the relative few who listen to public affairs programing.

The inattention of the viewing public to anything which is not entertainment or a news event of high dramatic content is a limiting factor in television's impact on the electorate. During the campaign of 1964, when the abyss between President Johnson and Senator Goldwater was considered sufficiently awesome to stir the population from its apathy, the campaign speeches of both candidates aroused scarcely a ripple in the ratings. Both were regularly outdrawn by westerns, situation comedies, and medical dramas—and by wide margins at that.

On election nights there is no choice, however, and the entire nation watches the returns as television performs, far more efficiently, the task which was once the newspapers'. In 1960, for the first time, television emerged as an incipient factor in the voting itself, and by 1964 the debate over this aspect of its influence was in full cry. By means of computers, and as a result of the three hours' time difference between the coasts, the competing networks are able to predict the ultimate result while West Coast voters are still on their way to the booths. Whether that constitutes undue influence has stirred a debate unique in American political life.

The networks have been quick to answer this possibly damaging charge with surveys which show that voters were not influenced in the election of 1964. But it may well be a mistake to accept this as fact. There is, indeed, a vast confusion in America between surveys and fact. "A survey shows . . ." is too often taken as final proof of a contention. In the case of television influence, it is quite possible that this is something sampling techniques cannot really measure, notwithstanding that those with a vested interest in them regard them as infallible. In any case, it is much too soon to come to a definite conclusion about this newest advance, if it is one, in American political life.

The speed of this advance has been incredible. In 1960, according to an NBC executive, "the computer was just a novelty . . . a machine down on Wall Street we cut to now and then." Four years later, in Studio 8-H, which the network had

built for Toscanini, $3 million worth of electronic data process-
ing equipment, the largest assemblage of computers ever in-
stalled in one room, was engaged in the competitive projection and analysis of election returns.

Computers of the future, as polltakers and technologists
learn to make and manipulate them better, may well be able,
on the basis of preliminary information, to predict the outcome
of elections with nearly 100 percent accuracy before voters
anywhere can get to the polls.

Only yesterday this idea was thought to be an absurdity. Today it is within reach technically, and it could produce the
first major conflict between the man-oriented society we have
always known and the machine society we are creating, a
conflict perhaps more important than technological unemployment. The ultimate triumph of television, with its instant access to all, or nearly all, the people, would be to harness this
medium with computer technology and the techniques of communications research to make the actions of the electorate a
foregone conclusion. Nominating conventions and elections
would only confirm what the machines had already concluded
and broadcast to the voters before they ever cast their ballots.
With the present 4 percent margin of possible error reduced by
improved techniques, even that shadowy hope of human re-
versal would disappear.

Impossible! the mind says; they would never permit it. But
would "they" prohibit by law the business of polltaking, the
business of news broadcasting, the business of computer analysis, all members in good standing of the free enterprise system?
One doubts it. Man's technology is advancing so rapidly he can
scarcely believe what he is doing, but another dozen years may
confront us squarely with at least one of the things we have
done as the traditional mechanics of the democratic system face
obsolescence.

If this is to be the end result of the interaction between politics and the mass media, television will have accomplished what
these media have been trying to do with varying success since
they were invented, which is to influence and in some degree

control the movements of society, particularly politics. They have been remarkably successful in the past, bearing in mind the relative proportions of "mass" and the mechanical limitations of the media.

It is possible to discover in the beginnings of the republic a prime example of the effective interaction between politics and one of the media. When the forces of the Revolution were gathering, it became the mission of the partisan patriot press to draw together the disparate threads of revolt. Those in the seaport towns needed little urging. The King's tax collectors were under their noses and the King's troops were sleeping in their beds, while the royal governors supererogated the power of the provincial assemblies. But the tide of population had already spilled over the Appalachians into the back country, where frontier necessity and physical removal made the inhabitants much less urgently concerned with the passions of Boston, New York, and Philadelphia.

Into this communications gap stepped the patriot provincial newspapers, circulating their publications everywhere postboys, barges, canoes, and travelers could carry them, and uniting revolution-minded men everywhere, as much as they could be united. True, the means the newspapers used were sometimes partisan lies and inflammatory, demagogic words, but the results were salutary.

A negative case could be made for the political influence of the press in the decades following the Revolution, for certainly the vicious partisan papers of what is often called the Dark Ages of American Journalism did as much to divide the population as anything occurring between the Revolution and the Civil War. More than that, the deep-lying passions separating Federalists and Jeffersonians have never cooled. They were at the core of the Johnson-Goldwater arguments in 1964, kept alive for more than a century and a half by generations of editors and political writers who would not let them die. Would they have died if the media had not existed? No one can know, but certainly the dissemination of political ideas to the American masses has been the principal product of our communications system, which is the largest and most effective the world has ever known.

That system reached its first peak of real effectiveness in the Civil War. Harriet Beecher Stowe may not have been in fact "the little lady who started the great war," as Lincoln is said to have called her, but there is no question that *Uncle Tom's Cabin* and the overwhelming quantity of Abolitionist literature which appeared in book and magazine form in the decade before Fort Sumter did more, perhaps, than anything else to arouse and focus northern opinion. Nor can the newspapers of both sides be minimized in their assault day after day on the minds and ·hearts of a people, already preconditioned to the basic elements of this dispute by the bitter division in the press for generations over Federalist and states' rights principles.

Lincoln himself owed his nomination to a pair of newspaper publishers, Charles Ray and Joseph Medill, of the *Chicago Tribune*. And on the road from there to the White House the most influential newspapers in the nation sold him to the voters, an action some of them lived to regret when, as President, he insisted on being his own man.

No adequate measure of the influence of the media on Civil War politics has ever been made, but we know it was considerable. The Copperhead press, for example, caused the Administration acute embarrassment and near disaster at a critical period in the war as a result of the Vallandigham case. The clamor of the press was, at least in part, responsible for McClellan's removal. The newspapers were, in fact, so intimately involved with the conduct of the war that for the first time censorship of the medium became a major issue, after Sherman's indignant threat to shoot correspondents who disclosed military information in their reports.

One must remember too that in the Civil War period newspapers and magazines were allies, and that magazines like *Harper's* were fully as influential as any newspaper. It is noteworthy, however, that the most significant political failure of the media occurred in the nation's largest city in 1864, where neither newspapers nor magazines could reach the blind prejudices of the Irish and German working class who had never been sympathetic to the Union cause and feared their jobs would be taken by freed Negroes. The city's most virulent Copperhead newspaper, Benjamin Wood's *Daily News* (not related to the present paper of the same name), fed the fears and bigotries of these masses, and substantial papers like Horace Greeley's *Tribune* and Henry J. Raymond's *Times* could do nothing to prevent the explosion of the bloody draft riots of 1864, one of the most shameful episodes in our political history.

It is ironic that one of the near victims of the murderous mob's anger was Greeley, whose *Tribune* had done so much to influence and support the cause of the nation's nonurban have nots, the farmers. Greeley had been the first national mouthpiece of the proletarian movement originating in the grassroots press of Kentucky which had propelled Andrew Jackson into the White House, the forerunner of nearly a century of agrarian revolt. As a candidate, Greeley's political aspirations proved to be abortive and in the end fatal to him, but his influence on the country's farmers through the *Tribune*, while not evident in the ballot boxes, nevertheless laid a solid foundation for the Populist movement later in the century.

For those of us who live in a time of the print media's declining political influence, it is becoming difficult to remember that it ever was so potent a factor in national politics that it was a serious matter to politicians which newspaper and magazine supported them, and that this concern was directly reflected in votes. "The warmongering press" is a cliché of the socialist camp around the world, but no one except dedicated fanatics seriously believes that the newspaper and magazine press could really inspire a war today. It is decidedly improbable that they ever had that much power.

For years it has been commonly believed by most people except historians that the Spanish-American War was a classic example of such a press-inspired war, and William Randolph Hearst, with his often-quoted telegram to Frederic Remington, "You get the pictures, I'll furnish the war," has been held up for decades as proof of the mass media's ability to influence national politics even as far as a declaration of war. President McKinley is customarily depicted as giving in to the demand for war by the press, led by the yellow journalism of the Hearst papers.

Aside from the doubtful authenticity of Hearst's telegram, there is little to support this theory. In scholarly studies of the war, and in modern general histories of the United States, Hearst is not even a footnote, and the role of the press becomes no more than that of a mouthpiece for a people suffused with the illusion of manifest destiny. The war in Cuba was considerably more complex in its origins, and America's entry was not influenced in a substantial way by the noisy outcries of the jingoist press.

Much more could be said for the considerable pressures brought to bear by the media in molding and crystallizing national sentiment for war in 1917—another of history's ironies, inasmuch as American newspapers and magazines had been generally so pro-German before submarine warfare began that the Allies at first refused to accredit American correspondents, and they were compelled to cover the war from the German side. The sudden switch to an hysterical clamor for war was an excellent example of how the press has, from time to time, capitalized on the surging flow of public emotion. Whether in this case it was the leader or the led is difficult to say.

In any event, the first World War was the last high water mark of the printed media's influence on American politics. That influence has been steadily receding ever since, with perhaps one notable exception. The rise of Herbert Hoover to the White House between 1919 and 1928 was guided and promoted by two of the most influential editors in America, but only one of them represented the mass media. As editor of *The Saturday Evening Post*, George Horace Lorimer was a powerful figure, although quite unknown to most people. He edited a magazine which had the highest circulation of any American periodical, and whose editorials, which Lorimer wrote anonymously, enjoyed an unprecedented national acceptance, not only by *Post* readers but by millions of other people who heard them quoted from pulpits and read them reprinted in other magazines and newspapers.

It was Lorimer's conviction as early as 1919 that Mr. Hoover would make a splendid President, and in this he was joined by William Allen White, whose Emporia *Gazette* was only a small Kansas newspaper but whose editorial voice was probably the most widely quoted in that medium. As backstage movers in the Republican Party, Lorimer and White used their publications, particularly the *Post*, to generate the enthusiasm for Mr. Hoover which led to his nomination and election. It is a typical political footnote to history that both men were disillusioned by their candidate after he was in office.

The influence of individual publishers and editors in the mass media has more than once been responsible for the nomination of Presidents. Lincoln's case can be compared with that of Franklin D. Roosevelt, who owed his nomination in 1932 to William Randolph Hearst. Although Hearst soon came to hate everything Mr. Roosevelt stood for, at the moment of crisis in the 1932 convention, when the New York governor faced defeat by the two thirds rule if there was another ballot, the publisher delivered to him the decisive convention votes he controlled because the alternative, so he believed, would be the nomination of Newton D. Baker, a corporation lawyer who had been a proponent of the League of Nations, both anathema to Hearst.

There has not been a similar instance since, and quite possibly there will never be another. Hearst was the last of the individual giants in the mass media, which are now controlled by boards of directors and management "teams." Moreover, newspapers themselves are not important influences politically, except in local situations where crusading papers still attack and occasionally root out corruption in city politics. Newspapers are business institutions today, dependent on advertising rather than on circulation as in the past, and like all the media whose lifeblood is advertising, they tend to reflect the attitudes and beliefs of the business community.

The beginnings of the decline in newspaper influence during the twenties and thirties was coincident with the rise of radio and television—media which developed an entirely different pattern of interaction with the political scene. Where newspapers and magazines used the weapon of crusade and individual attack against politicians and their actions, the weapon of television was exposure. Television, however, did not regard exposure as a weapon because it was not on the attack. It was simply in a competitive race with itself to show the public as much as it profitably could on the home screen.

To understand the difference, one need only compare the political scene of 1906-07 with that of today. In the era of trust-busting under President Theodore Roosevelt, the assault on the iniquities of monopoly was led by muckraking magazines like *McClure's*, and by individual muckrakers like Ida Tarbell, whose exposé of Standard Oil became a landmark of its kind. Together, writers and magazines aroused the public sentiment which supported the reform programs of Roosevelt, helped to split the Republican Party in 1912, and laid a floor of public support under the reformer Woodrow Wilson.

It was, furthermore, great crusading newspapers like the New York *World* which did not hesitate to attack the United States Senate itself in 1909-10. David Graham Phillips' articles, "The Shame of the Senate," exposing the unholy alliance between Standard Oil and certain Senators, aroused the whole nation and led to the dissolution by court decision of the company's monopoly and effectively ended its illicit influence in Congress.

Today no newspaper is capable of creating such national indignation. There are far too many Americans, constantly exposed to far too many competing communications voices, for any single newspaper or magazine to exercise such influence on the voters. Corruption in these days is attacked by newspapers largely for partisan political advantage, as in the Bobby Baker case, and not for the purpose of exposing the deep nonpolitical corruption lying beneath. Corruption itself is an industry in the United States, almost too big to be attacked at all.

By contrast with the muckraking era, the influence of the dominant medium today, television, is directed not toward social criticism but to the processing and display of largely noneditorial information. A few network documentaries, like *The Making of a President*, make editorial points directly or indirectly, and some comments create serious trouble with sponsors, who are reluctant to buy any program with a point of view. Documentaries and network news commentary programs, with few exceptions, are devoted mostly to exposing the viewer to an amount of information circumscribed by the network's ability to sell such programs and its willingness to devote good time to public service programing. Exposure is the keynote, too, in the several shows on which public figures are interviewed. On these shows the editorial viewpoint is never introduced. The public is invited by implication to arrive at its own opinion after the subject and its current beliefs have been examined. Usually the subject does not say anything of significance, but there is merit in this approach because the nature of television often makes the exposure a revelation of character.

The overall effect, however, of the interaction between politics and the mass media today is one of blandness. The tremendous growth of these media, concurrent with the explosion of population, has resulted in the impersonal ambience which the word "mass" implies. Masses are composed of many people with differing opinions, ideas, and prejudices. Mass media, if they are to reach these people, must either appeal to them across the broadest possible spectrum of opinion or else by advancing no opinion at all, simply presenting information as entertainment. The latter is easier.

Television is, obviously, the most effective way ever designed to reach great masses of people. Already it can supply an audience of more than fifty million people at once in the United States with instant information, and when the satellite communciations system is fully established, the number of viewers who can be summoned to look at a single political figure on the screen is limited theoretically only by the number of those who own television sets, a figure which is increasing astronomically.

Naturally there are speculation and controversy about what the arrival of global television will mean to politics at home and abroad. Will it be the relatively nonpolitical kind of broadcasting Americans have become accustomed to, on a cooperative basis, or will it be a free-for-all propaganda barrage, as so many nations use their national television outlets now? The possibilities for new international understanding are self-evident, but so too are the more realistic prospects of self-serving nationalism on the largest possible scale.

Paradoxically, the prospect of this ultimate broadening of the mass media—with implications for film, magazines, and newspapers as well—imposes a new responsibility on the individual in a democratic society. Heads of state and legislators will still be elected by ballot, presumably, and systems of government, no matter how they may be altered, will still represent a political process adapted to the needs and desires of the individual country. Every word that is spoken on global television, heard on international radio, or read in one of the print media must be written somewhere by human hands, transmitting the ideas which originate in human brains. Computers may be capable of writing mechanically, but presumably they can never think in the way the human brain thinks. To the proposition advanced by some scientists that there is no theoretical reason why machines cannot be built which will entirely duplicate the action of the human brain, one can only ask what rational reason exists for doing so, unless man is truly determined to make himself obsolete.

We must proceed on the assumption that political institutions, and society itself, will remain in the hands of thinking human beings. If that is so, the responsibility of the educator takes on a new and more profound meaning. Words which were once confined to the local newspaper, the national magazine, or the American television network will have a global impact, with consequences difficult to measure. The need for clear and logical thinking and writing, already acute, will be far greater, in proportion to their potential total effect. Consequently the entire educational system, from top to bottom, will (or should be) concerned with the use of language, spoken and written, and with the uses of ideas. Populations which are able to understand political situations and to express themselves adequately through their leaders will be the keepers of the future. Since these situations are certain to become increasingly complex, there is a corresponding need to train people for the mass media who will be capable of translating complicated ideas into clear and understandable terms—who will, in brief, be capable of explaining the world to the people who live in it.

Traditionally we are people who gain our knowledge through the written word, and there is still much to be done in smoothing the path between writer and reader. But we must now begin to train people in the visual and aural absorption of knowledge, and teach them how to relate what they see and hear to what they read, for there is no reason to believe, as some communications extremists contend, that the printed word will be obsolete. Techniques of selectivity and judgment are called for, areas of background knowledge must be built, against which will be projected the political ideas people are subjected to by global television.

The alternative to this kind of education would be chaos. An electorate unable to understand or absorb the multiple worldwide images of television will be unequipped to contend with the profound changes in political institutions which inevitably lie ahead. The lag in this respect is already making itself evident in the disparity between present realities and obsolete patterns of political thought in America and elsewhere. If there is to be rational political discourse in this country and the world, there is no real alternative to the education of people in the meaning and many uses of the spoken and written word.

It is a supreme challenge to which educators may well address themselves, if not with complete confidence in the outcome, at least with a sense of the vital, probably decisive, importance of their mission.

Jack Behar

On Rod Serling, James Agee, and Popular Culture

Arthur Miller had some trouble convincing us of the moral authenticity, let alone the tragic stature, of Willy Loman in *Death of a Salesman*, a very self-conscious modern morality play, conceived—so it seems—to invite a highly charged identification followed by heavy seizures of *mea culpa*. Whatever the play's faults may be, Miller's effort to get into it a typical case of American self-displacement was a plainly ambitious one. Rod Serling and Paddy Chayefsky, in *Requiem for a Heavyweight* and *Marty*, follow Miller in the attempt to explore (or perhaps, more aptly, to celebrate) the moral universe of the common man: Serling to dramatize the pathos of an all but silent affliction suffered by a loveless and sexless ex-prize fighter; Chayefsky to affirm the claims of love modestly conceived. There was some necessary ambiguity in Miller's treatment of Loman; on certain assumptions, at least, it was hard to tell whether Loman's dreams were of the stuff that makes a man a culture-hero or a scapegoat. In any case, Miller's need to offer psychological explanations in Willy's behalf gave us the clue to the difficulty of writing American morality plays in a diluted "social protest" vein.

By contrast with Miller, Serling and Chayefsky are surer of their ground, much less ambitious. Both take pride in their professionalism, of course, and Chayefsky talks sometimes as if he were conducting a course in Television Play Writing I. Only in a very marginal and oblique way do Serling and Chayefsky challenge the values we are told we live by; perhaps their prudence is not necessarily a fault—the fate of real challenges, not to mention the difficulty of conceiving them, being what it is nowadays. In *Requiem for a Heavyweight* Serling's gross intention is to write a television play in something of a celebratory mode: to represent a good if witless man—submerged in the stereotype of the prize fighter and treated as an object—who becomes the victim of the prize-fighting racket and the soft-hard mindedness of those who run it, especially Maish and the mob behind him. In *Marty*, Chayefsky's aim was to lovingly evoke, by way of certain gently humorous formulas of speech and gesture, the world of a Bronx neighborhood, and to represent his hero's break with it as he submits at last to the claims of love. Decently modest in conception, attractively stylized, *Marty* was persuasive and touching as a representative anecdote, as a fable handed down by a local colorist that belongs to the folklore of love in the Bronx.

Chayefsky tells us that he took pains to get the dialogue right: he wanted to get as close to "literal reality" as possible, so he studied the speech of actual people. Serling studied the fight crowd, especially the "ghosts" who drift helplessly in and out of it; and we can assume, I think, that he was possessed by a need to celebrate, perforce somewhat sentimentally, the all but anonymous victims—the Mountains of that familiarly strange world. Both Serling and Chayefsky are committed, then, as one would expect, to the realistic television play, and they speak as devoted literalists of the imagination, hoping to get the exactness of reportage—the anthropological exactitude of gesture and movement—into their work. They write, as it turns out, heavily stylized and sentimentalized quasi-documentary plays, beginning with the available stereotypes and then proceeding to turn them upside down. In *Requiem for a Heavyweight*, for example, the question is: Can Mountain be saved from the stereotype that already has all but consumed him? Or: Can Mountain be saved from Maish, the father-figure who has all but unsexed him? The answer the television play gives is somewhat evasive, since although Mountain cannot quite be saved from Maish, the hope is that he might come to save himself by administering something of his sheer animal goodness to deprived children.

The major virtue of the television play (one wholly absent from the movie adaptation)[1] is that it forces on us the sheer presence of Maish, Army, and Mountain in an overwhelmingly physical way. Speaking face to face, crowding out almost everything Serling brings into the film adaptation, they fill the screen, they command our attention, and they are held to their mythic types. This is not the case with the movie; things spread dangerously thin, so that most of the anxiety-filled moments of the television play are wholly lost. We lose, above all, the slow, deftly uncertain melancholy of Ed Wynn, Mountain's trainer, which is replaced by the studied gloominess of Mickey Rooney, who manages hardly more than a plain man's inarticulateness in the face of moral evil. In the television version, Wynn provides something like a choral commentary on the action in his brave, uncertain responses and his utterly helpless brooding, and it is this which gives some dramatic substance to the "ritual" character of the action. (One feels that Ed Wynn's acting in the television version was a wonderfully happy accident.) The television play is uncluttered by Serling's later unhappy inventions, so that the "requiem" for Mountain has a chance to sound out cleanly and intensely within the limits set by a modestly small initiating idea, but one with the force behind it of our obsessive interest in the fight game and the mythical life of the exhausted pug. The quite incredible scenes in the movie adaptation—inserted to pep things up, no doubt—in which Ma, the threatening lesbian mobster, appears, are more than enough to strain to the breaking point any attempt to approximate "literal reality." In the television play we never see Mr. Henson, the gangster patriarch who threatens Maish's life—only his lackeys. It is enough that one of the lackeys appears to make credible the force his boss commands: he nails Maish's hand down to the floor with his shoe and grinds the lesson in, so to speak. In the movie, on the other hand, Ma appears in the odd

---

[1] The movie version is available for screening in 16 mm.

disguise of a reject do-it-yourself Gestapo officer, ready to over-
see the sadomasochistic carnage, her lesbian pulchritude concealed beneath the heavy sexless leer. Her (his) presence
appears to be a bad joke, as one might conclude charitably;
nonetheless, the utterly phony scenes in which Ma figures
undercut the relevant drama of the movie (thin to begin with),
shifting the emphasis to the visible lesbian, sadomasochistic
world behind it. Why one needs this world brought to visible
life, only Columbia Pictures can tell us.

The obvious contrivances in the film version are to be interpreted not only as Serling's attempt to "fill out" the television
scenario, but also as an effort to toughen it. The rather sentimental ending of the television play that has Mountain going
home to Tennessee hopefully to be reborn, his dignity still intact, is replaced by the scenes which give us his final degradation; he enters the ring, burdened by his knowledge of what he
must do, and finally yields up the ghost in whooping like a good
Indian—a dead Indian. This conclusion is made almost inevitable by a sequence of action, the ineptness of which I find quite
inexplicable, a breakdown in Hollywood professionalism. I am
referring to the strange sequence that shatters whatever right-
ness of design the dramatic action might conceivably have had:
Maish's getting Mountain drunk at Jack Dempsey's (Dempsey
and Gleason together at a table tell us all we need to know
about the ambience of the movie), the pathetic failure of Mountain's effort to find a new life, and Maish's final meeting with
Grace. The whole sequence, of course, is designed to bring
Mountain into the ring as a whooping Indian wrestler, and this
is more transparent than it has any right to be. What should
appear to be a struggle for Mountain's soul becomes instead
merely an excuse to impose what Serling apparently considers
to be a tragic conclusion. Maish confronts Grace, telling her
in a display of deadly honesty, that she should leave Mountain
to the end that Maish (and, as it were, the fates) has engineered for him. Strangely enough, Maish's plea that Grace
stop feeding Mountain illusions about the future silences her
immediately, although all that Grace has been doing is trying

to secure Mountain a modest sort of job in a boys' camp. Presumably the point is that Maish, in his confused and unacknowledged love for Mountain, must impose the final humiliation because he knows that Mountain can never live in the humdrum world Grace would have him enter. Of course Maish needs Mountain if he is to save his own life, so that it is not easy to make sense of his final act of honesty. If we are to take the honesty seriously, then he should not seem to be playing God so as to save himself from the mob; whereas he appears to be doing precisely this. After the meeting with Maish, Grace disappears, and Mountain is left to negotiate as best he can with Maish.

On the whole, what is merely hokum in the movie—Ma and her gang, Mountain's getting drunk, the one violent brawl we have at the end—tends to overshadow what is modestly decent in it, the middle section that is concerned with the small romance between Mountain and Grace. The conclusion is very dubiously contrived; after Mountain is confronted with Maish's imminent end, there is little he can do except get his manager out of hock to the underworld. We are apt to think that what becomes Mountain's fate is shaped merely by necessities which Serling had to satisfy: the need to fill out a television script that wanted toughening, toughening easily provided by a dose or two of violence, a tease of straight lesbianism, and at least the possibility visually registered of Maish's getting stomped on by the gangland gestapo.

Beneath the obvious failures of the movie version exist attitudes which, unexamined and self-perpetuating, seem dangerously shallow and complacent. The clue, I believe, is in some words Serling writes in the preface to the "reading version" of the film script as a dedication to a lost world he once knew:

> To the Mountain Riveras—to the punchies, the cauliflowered wrecks, the mumbling ghosts of Eighth Avenue's bars, the dancing masters of another time who now walk on rubber legs. To the has-beens, the never-weres, the also-rans—this book is dedicated with affection and respect.

These are not unimpressive clichés, although, on the other hand, it is not unimaginable that a Walter Winchell could have done as well by the "Mountain Riveras." The carefully processed New Yorkese makes "affection and respect" hard to come by. There exists in the language the sign of an easily spent emotional identification, self-serving, hardly self-effacing, in fact merely a form of attitudinizing. And the attitudinizing exhibited here, furthermore, compromises the realism that Serling would be faithful to, which becomes, in effect, a veneer under which is concealed lazily nostalgic feeling and a thin curiosity. Serling probably felt pity for Mountain Rivera, but all the respect he can show him is to impose upon him the burden of being a sacrificial hero, which is after all small tribute to one's respect, particularly so when what we need so badly is the man himself. We get, therefore, only another form of distortion and idealization; the warm feelings toward the "cauliflowered wrecks" end, predictably, in abstraction.

Presumably the intent of both the television play and the movie version is to rescue "the mumbling ghosts," to bring them back alive from the lower depths of Broadway, not only to enact their "requiem." That is to say, to restore them, not to bury them in abstraction and hokum and ritual sacrifice— certainly not to make the sacrifice the measure of their dignity. The problem Serling faces but cannot solve, apparently, is what to do with Mountain after he has brought him back to life in the scenes with Grace. In the television play, Serling has finally to send him back to Tennessee; in the movie version, he makes him into a victim, but a victim who is somehow a hero, a sadly sentimental paradox. It is to be identified, I think, with the tough-guy sentimentality of Broadway, the notion that underneath a hard surface crust everyone is a man of good feeling, or could be if only he did not always have to be on his guard lest the world cave in on him. Maish is the exemplar here, a man of essentially good feeling who finds himself hopelessly caught as he desperately tries to stay alive in a mean world.

What saves the movie version from being a total failure as an attempt to save the man from the stereotype, to restore him to *our* world, is that it succeeds in telling us what Mountain's world has been like: not merely impoverished by Mountain's incapacity for words and the usual *ersatz* masculine camaraderie, but loveless, sexless, empty beyond the emptiness of those who use Mountain. In the television play, Ed Wynn speaks the word "love," unlike Mickey Rooney in the movie adaptation, who seems never more than routinely depressed by the spectacle of Maish's evil-doings and merely at a loss for what to say. Except for the one utterance of the uneasy word, we have only the inevitable expressions of tough-guy nostalgia in the style the movies have made popular, the communication so stylized as to all but disappear into the clichés which collapse it into parody. So the scenes in the movie version between Grace and Mountain give us, by contrast, something very different: personal communication that at last brings Mountain to life—and here Anthony Quinn as Mountain sets a finely controlled awkwardness to work against Grace's astonishing interest in him. The point the movie makes is that personal communication and the concomitant awakening of the spirit, even at this rudimentary level, have no chance against the world in which men bide their time in old Broadway hotels. The scene between Mountain and Grace is well conceived, touching and serious beneath the confused play of words; but its excellence is soon swamped by the crudeness and artificiality of what follows. Ma comes back to life, and we move finally to Mountain's disgraceful yelping and the pseudo-sacrificial end.

For all the effort to duplicate the real world of the prize fighter—one thinks of the location scenes shot in New York City—there is little sense of a real world in the movie, and what there is gives way to the unusual vulgarity of so much that is offered in place of the real world. One ends by attending to one's own amazed incredulity. A curious premise of the film seems to be that a "real" Jack Dempsey talking to a "real" Jackie Gleason puts us one up on the road to realism. It is likely, rather, to put us one down on the road to the chummy intramuralism of the Hollywood-New York entertainment axis, to a ludicrous overestimation of what "real" faces contribute to a drama that is already in danger of being overstylized and that certainly is harmed by the veneer of Hollywood unprofessionalism painted over it. The veneer, as I have said, is pierced in a quite unbelievable fashion by Ma and her boys, a violation that is enough to sink the film, I should think. That it is not wholly sunk is the work of Anthony Quinn who, although he is now and then on the edge of falling into a too exaggerated pathetic dopiness, manages to be exhilarating in bringing alive something of Mountain's submerged and unsatisfied needs, which are the needs, after all, of everyone.

What we needed in the television play was a fuller exploration of these needs, not simply the standard, needlessly timid recognition that they exist. The television play, that is to say, lacked sex, repressing therefore the main issue, which in the film adaptation Serling makes some effort to represent in the scene between Mountain and Grace at the end of the movie. All that comes of it, however, is in the good-girl lines which Grace speaks to Maish: "I just think the next thing he wanted he should have gotten—I wish to God it were something I could have given to him." Thus is prepared the necessary fade-out, and so fades out too a belated effort to focus the small disabling human fear and repression next to which the contrived sacrificial end is of literally no importance. This opportunity missed, all that we can get is a none too interesting exercise in the analysis of a corrupt and corrupting ritual dramatically generalized. What we hope to have explored openly is the relation between the ordinary enough pathos of disgraced manhood, the loss of meaning, the victimization of Mountain's primitive loyalty, and—beneath these—the sexless, all-too-masculine, all-too-repressive world in which Mountain has lived his life. If Mountain is not to be seen as a good simple sort who goes willingly to the slaughter, his loyalty to Maish simply the product of his mindlessness, Serling must rise to an honorable treatment of sex. But he does not. He feeds Mountain to the slaughter.

Between the faces and bodies that register wildly and beautifully for a moment in the television play and the astonishing ineptness of so much in the movie adaptation, it is not hard to choose. The television camera keeps the world small, claustrophobic, intensely inane, as it were, while the big screen merely invites the hokum that, in retrospect, seemed rather predictable. On the one hand, there is the dark, exaggerated largeness of things in the television play, the product of a style that can descend of course into a familiar kind of artiness; and on the other, a hopeless, depressing stiffness: Jackie Gleason's climactic well-rehearsed wide-eyed fear and Mickey Rooney's poker-faced commiseration. In the end, then, we have a realized aliveness, spontaneity, a sense of real bodies, some closeness of design, in the television play, and only dourness, easy evil, stiffness, mock brutality, in the movie adaptation. The television play triumphs precisely because it is necessarily obedient to the relatively narrow frame of things imposed by the television camera, and hence it remains uncorrupted by pseudo-realistic excess and unwitting parody. There is no Jack Dempsey to introduce us into his restaurant, and no Jackie Gleason who has likely been in it from time to time. The movie adaptation, in contrast, extends but does not intensify—indeed, thins and flattens out—what we have in the television play, and except perhaps for the initial sequence which we get from the point of view of the defeated Mountain, it is visually uninteresting, more dead than alive.

II

The effort of the American writer to treat "everyday reality" responsibly is tied up with a question I believe crucial to the whole problem of popular culture in our day—the question of realism: a complex question with an interesting history in America. I want first to look backward to Emerson and Whitman, in a nineteenth century prophetic voice; then forward to Van Wyck Brooks, Paul Rosenfeld, and Waldo Frank, reinstating the prophetic voice during the first decades of the twentieth century, only now more urgently; and finally at attitudes toward mass culture with which we are familiar.

It was of course one of the great hopes of Emerson and Whitman—as of those who tried heroically to act on their hopes during the early decades of our century—that an American literature would arise which would take ordinary reality as its inescapable province, that it would make us one with "the spirit of the place" as it created an American type of the imagination. In "The American Scholar" Emerson spoke of "the meal in the firkin, the milk in the pan" as necessary objects of literary representation, in contrast, say, to patently un-American objects of a sublime or tragic order. "The near, the low, the common" were to be exalted, set firmly into the literary record—possibly transfigured by the operations of intense scrutiny and live Spirit. Imminent Spirit was to be witnessed, in fact, in all its grandeur in the abounding factuality of American life. As Emerson and Whitman hoped, so they spoke, fashioning a romantic metaphysics in a prophetic mode, one that could comfortably extend to what Whitman celebrated in 1871 as a "New World metaphysics." A good many books have been written in America since Emerson spoke of the duties of his priestly elect; and although we still worry about the American identity, the fact is that we have identified the writers who give us the terms out of which we construct an American type of the imagination—or at least an American type of the primordial Adam.[2] There is little mystery today concerning the shape of our major American myth.

There may yet be some mystery remaining, however, about "the near, the low, the common," treacherous and ambiguous territory for the writer, as about what (hoping to identify it) we call "everyday reality," "the common reality," and extending the terms, "the common man." There was no such unyielding mystery for Emerson. Emersonian transcendentalism was based upon the premise that each man, if only he would come to live vitally enough, could come to know himself as one with the common reality: "that common nature which it is the

---

[2] For an historical treatment of the use American writers have made of the image of the new Adam, see R. W. B. Lewis, *The American Adam* (Chicago: University of Chicago Press, 1955).

dearest desire of all to see enlarged and glorified." Hopefully, he could come to know in his own experience something of the express need of the poet to transfigure the natural world, something of the relentless "drenching" of experience to which the poet was dedicated in his magnificent effort to make the visible world a world that administered to the needs of man. And for Emerson, of course, the visible world was the handiwork of God, necessarily emblematic, inhabited by Spirit, from which man could come to intuit the divine oneness of things in the universe—the order in which and from which he literally takes his life. The final hope, in effect, was that a transcendentalism of the priestly elite could become an attitude toward experience shared by the people, that the ordinary or commonplace could be transfigured within the patterns of everyday thought and action, that man could live an exalted life as he responded vitally to the minute variegated world in which he found himself.

Of course, Emerson's passionate declaiming against a timid reliance on the culture of the past—which Whitman inherits—and his attempt to inspire fresh observation of the near-at-hand are always somewhat compromised by his ever present knowledge that the near-at-hand can be transcendentalized—that it yields to the work of Spirit. In the passage, for example, in which we find "I embrace the common, I explore and sit at the feet of the familiar, the low," the phrases "ultimate reason," "the highest spiritual cause," and "eternal Law" occur. Emerson never thought that the delineation of living process in the quotidian world would be the proper end of poetry. External nature, justly appreciated, could offer evidence of ultimate law, of the divine order of things in the world. Emerson soon gets us around to Swedenborg, and it is depressing, really, that nature should be valued only insofar as it can be conceived as the "correspondence" of Soul or Spirit, as emblematic, as inserted into a metaphysics.

Of course, Emerson was not working out the model of a popular culture for his day, although there is enough in his writings to suggest he might have been inclined to do so if only his transcendentalism let him. He was writing at the beginning

of developments that in our day have become the subject both
of occasional moralists and of scholar-critics. He is nothing if not
the archetype of the poet-preacher-educator whose ambiguous
task has become to torment us into discovering a Self, armed
against *kitsch*, able to withstand the assaults aimed at us from
the mass society. The American literature Emerson looked forward to was conceived to be in some sense a popular literature:
one that would be hospitable to the quotidian world, to the
low and ordinary. Yet the distance from Emerson and Whitman
to the electronic media and the new mass culture is a fright-
fully long distance; "modernism" in the arts has signally inter-
vened, for one thing, and with it have followed those agonizing
inventories of our crisis so typical of our time, all of them
pointing to the obvious truth that we have suffered our unfortunate fall into the mass society, where the exegesis demanded
of us must seek to comprehend the new forms of culture that
greet us at every turn: forms not necessarily generous, sane,
and fraternal, nor rapturously bardic, Emersonian, and democratic.

There is a growing awareness that the returns grow increasingly thin on essays whose sole intention is to interpret the
pathology of mass culture: to show us how we can come to
resist mass culture so as to save ourselves. Critics who assume
(often with little if any presumptive evidence) that mass culture gives a fair reflection of the lives of other people, but are
themselves seldom if ever engaged by what is alive in the popular art forms, end in a steely abstractionist stupor. They are
doomed to appear as dead (and deadening to us) as what provides them the occasion for exercise in a standard form of modern polemic. One's point of view is obviously important. One
can examine mass culture as one examines a disease, and find
in it the identical worrisome features that belong to the received picture we have of industrialized societies. In doing so,
one typically ignores the appeal a given cultural product makes
and the form in which this is mediated. We learn how alienated
we are, how depersonalized our lives have become, how much
we stand in need of direct experience. Or one can examine

products of mass culture to discover how they support values that belong to the social structure. We learn how our consent is engineered, how the duplicities of our culture are put over on us. Or, like Dwight Macdonald, one can feel the need to protect a vulnerable cultural tradition from debasement in mass or middlebrow art, and write up witty accounts of the ways the debasement is registered.

In *Against the American Grain* (New York: Random House, 1962) Macdonald writes: "In the last two centuries, our traditional culture has been under increasing pressure from mass culture, a conflict which has reached its greatest intensity in this country." Unfortunately, little that is gritty or problematic finds a place in Macdonald's prose; the language is the ordinary passionless language of the cultural debate. It does not occur to Macdonald that to speak so confidently of "our traditional culture" is somewhat absurd, unless one thinks of culture, not as an ongoing affair constantly being modified, but in a rigid, possessive way, as made up, say, of a canon of the best books. Other voices in the debate have not sounded quite so confident; or at least they imagined other uses, besides those of good journalistic polemic, for their accounts. F. R. Leavis and Denys Thompson, in *Culture and Environment* (London: Chatto & Windus, 1933), did not think of "minority culture" as the possession of a few troubled protectionist spirits. They were too much concerned to develop methods of analysis and judgment of the new advertising-entertainment media; and at the same time they were arguing out, as it were, a syllabus of reading that would show how "minority culture" was to be preserved and extended in educational practice. Above all, of course, they were acting as educators; the modern syllabus was intended to help shape an imagination accessible to the possibilities of life. Indeed, "minority culture" was to be rescued from the minority into whose control it had devolved and made as relevant as possible to an environment shaped by mass literacy, advertising, and the new forms of popular culture. Macdonald, on the other hand, merely insists over and over again that the multitudinous processors among us have debased elite culture. And he refuses to take any notice at all of people whose needs are unsatisfied, or in fact frustrated, by elite culture in the form he would have it preserved and perpetuated. But few critics have been able to talk intelligently about needs.

In the United States it is not easy to talk long about "our traditional culture." This very prim phrase points to nothing very substantial. Is Greek Revival architecture, for example, part of "our traditional culture"? If we mean by it a body of art and general thought, and the values and standards linked with it, that can be rather easily sustained and communicated from generation to generation, or, as Malcolm Bradbury has put it, "a body of special experiences associated with persons whose taste and status are upheld by traditional sanctions," then it is apparently an overly thin notion, hardly applicable to American life. It is precisely the lack of a viable cultural tradition that many critics of mass culture find so damaging to elite art in America. Reuel Denney has shown us something of the history of this problem.[3] What the history of our thinking about it demonstrates is a strange paradox: former Trotskyists and intellectuals of the left, alarmed by the ubiquitousness of *kitsch* and the blurring of distinctions among works of art and in general thought, have completely jettisoned the vision of a new America—an America unified under the aspect of a new life of the imagination—that had precipitated the literary and political radicalism of the generation of Van Wyck Brooks during the years 1910 to 1930. Macdonald, for instance, wishes to have the separation between mass and elite made absolute so that no mongrel breed of art and thought can arise to discomfort him.

The hopes for American culture harbored by Van Wyck Brooks, Paul Rosenfeld, Lewis Mumford, and Waldo Frank, during roughly the first quarter of the century, were of an obviously different order and quality of feeling. They shared, as had Emerson and Whitman before them, what now appears

---

[3] See Reuel Denney, "The Discovery of the Popular Culture," in *American Perspectives*, ed. Robert Spiller and Eric Larrabee (Cambridge: Harvard University Press, 1961), pp. 154-177.

to be the extraordinary fantasy that a national sensibility could be created under the aegis of a "divine literatus," that American life would achieve some overreaching imaginative realization in art and literature. What gave Brooks and his followers their peculiarly attractive sense of mission, however, was not merely the common belief in the power of art to shape an American type of the imagination, but their all but mystical conviction that the poet who would "beat the rhythm of his age" could thereby act to unify an otherwise polarized, blindly acquisitive society and give it identity. A characteristic utterance is the following by Paul Rosenfeld:

> It is the poet alone who can bring all the faculties of life moving together and procure for life that all-pervasive style that is the condition of civilization. It is the poet alone who can make society take the shape which can satisfy the human soul. It is the poet alone who can end the schism in American men; can turn American life toward personal ends, and develop out of an anarchical competitive horde a community of men who give and enrich themselves in giving.[4]

And we can place next to it another by Waldo Frank:

> What we require of leadership is clearly an integration of our chaos: its rebirth into organic life by the introduction within it of a fresh germinal force. To this end, first of all, the chaos must be accepted; then, understood and transfigured. To accept is the work of the spirit: to understand is the work of mind: to transfigure is the work of art.[5]

The "rediscovery of America" was not to end, then, in simply the conquest of a "usable past": it was an effort to cut beneath the fatigue, the thinness, the increasing commercialization of American life, to discover a kind of permanently revolutionary ardor and fraternity of spirit that could stand against and ulti-

---

[4] Paul Rosenfeld, "Van Wyck Brooks," *Port of New York* (Urbana: University of Illinois Press, 1961 [New York, 1924]), p. 42.

[5] Waldo Frank, *The Rediscovery of America* (New York: Charles Scribner's Sons, 1929), p. 179.

mately transform a culture unable to nourish either the individual spirit or genuine community life. The tone of the writers
varied greatly. Waldo Frank's conception of the organic society,
his cultural mysticism, was emotionally charged sometimes to
the point of frenzy, while Brooks was hard, unremitting, and
magisterial in his estimates of the American past. But whatever their tone, all of the writers shared the belief that imaginative process could create the bonds of community: a national
idea and sensibility that could resolve the contradictions of
thought and action, disembodied spirit and hard materialism,
the effete and the plebeian. Of course, their radical vision of
American life was itself willed and desperate, for it envisaged
fundamental changes in an industrial order that had long been
undermining the world of Emerson and Whitman from which
they took their inspiration. Nonetheless, they had begun, as
Lewis Mumford put it in *The Golden Day* in 1926 (reissued;
Gloucester, Mass.: Peter Smith): "again to dream Thoreau's
dream—of what it means to live a whole human life." The
whole issue was cast, finally, in a somewhat melodramatic
form: the life-denying purism of mind or spirit as against the
"whole" man; the late disembodied Romantic spirituality of an
Edgar Allan Poe, say, as against a poetry that would "articulate
the whole life of the people"; a society disabled by its traditional divisiveness as against one drawn together into an organic whole. Here was the mysticism of the organic placed in
the service of Utopia.

The writers I have mentioned here, all too briefly, were indeed Utopians, generously hopeful, anything but niggardly and
afraid, imagining the final liberating wholeness that today we
are likely to snicker at. Certainly, they were greatly helped by
the loosening in American life coordinate with the advent of
"modernism" in the arts—with the discovery that modernism
was a joyous testament to human freedom and liberation. They
played very self-consciously a common historical role that now
seems impossible. The positive role has now been replaced by
the defensive posture, so that we are much given to the analysis
of teasing horrors of one kind or another. The analysis of mass

culture becomes a very smartly processed game, another empty
ritual shored up against our ruin, occupation enough during
the forced interregnum: when the protests we raise themselves
become problematic, when we do not know what we want,
when we helplessly protest again and again the debasement of
the language of the tribe, or the processing of further spurious
roles for us to play, or the sadomasochistic carnage that flashes
before our eyes for a terrible instant. The lifeline becomes whoever has some teasing metaphysical horror to peddle; or parody
raised upon parody, Camp upon expired Camp. We keep up
with the ways of the Enemy, enjoy our spurious alienation,
keep our fantasy life churning, look longingly for the appearance of the Apocalypse in the Picture Tube. And that is all.

Much of the criticism of mass culture has been disingenuous.
Mass culture interested us for the wrong reasons, because it
could all too easily be conceived of as another gross phenomenon of "modern life," as the gross sign of the Unfortunate Fall
into *kitsch*—into the soft horrors of American life. It allowed
for keeping abreast of the underworld of the American imagination without any disconcertingly serious commitments to the
real world, for gloating superciliously over the processed fantasies without, in James Baldwin's words, having to pay one's
dues. The point is that for all the sometimes deadly brilliance
of the criticism, it was somehow too detached, too cerebral, too
much the product of ready-made theory applied to an obviously
vulnerable art, too committed to a ready-made characterization
of the audience who would be inevitably used by those who
could not help but use the art wrongly. It simply gave us the
news of what soft catastrophes our century had so far pioneered. So now our task is to discover how we can pay our
dues, which might mean to newly envisage what genuine popular culture might be like, or at least to redefine our mutual
problems, as we meet—the Apocalypse not having quite de-
scended on us—on the safe side of hysteria and cultural despair.
Among these problems, as I suggest above, is the problem of
realism, a matter to which I shall return below.

Summing it up: During the first decades of the twentieth

century Van Wyck Brooks, using the old terms that today are so utterly problematic, had projected the shared hope for a truly national culture—as the saying had it, an "organic culture"—neither highbrow nor lowbrow, but assimilating the high spirituality of the New England writers and the new forms and energies manifest beneath the happy materialism of the country as a whole. In our own time, by contrast, the general view has been that a "middle culture" has proven a disaster, a parasitic feeding off the techniques of elite culture, with the consequence that debased elite culture is ground out according to recipe, the recipes called "story ideas." For Brooks the manifest energies in America were about to crystallize to provide an archetypally American expression of the imagination, all regional differences spent or happily absorbed. For someone like the late Richard Chase, whose book *The Democratic Vista* (Garden City: Doubleday & Co., 1958) is a key text in the cultural debate, on the other hand, the genius of American letters was to be sought in writers who embodied the contradictions of their culture and managed to keep from being absorbed into its soft middle way. The "organic culture" of the Utopians was a fine and happy myth, even a necessary one, but of little relevance during a time when the channels were crowded with processed elite culture. Beneath the writers whom he celebrated for their triumphantly oblique ironies and masks, in the middle culture created under the aegis, say, of a William Dean Howells, Chase could find little else than an unctuous, self-ingratiating, flabby culture for the affluent and comfortable middle class and a mass culture potentially vital but in any case relatively harmless. Given this tripartite picture, the responsibility of the American intellectual was clear; he was to champion the individualistic, unmalleable, radical vision of the classic American writers and, living without ideology, certainly without Utopia, be committed to the values of the avant-garde, now somewhat worn and timid, but of course the measure of the new desperation: irony, tension, contrariety—the rewards of unease lived through without the aid of nostrums and recipes.

After one has worked his way through the necessary attempts at theory and generalization, it is easy to want to hold in abeyance such terms as "traditional culture," "mass culture," "elite culture," "organic society," etc. One begins to think of them as offering false perspectives, as precipitating certain crisis-ridden formulas of severely limited utility. All the talk about mass culture will remain finally ghostly and arcane while we are preoccupied with the analysis of merely gross phenomena. Moreover, such analysis all too frequently merely hardens received ideas about "our crisis."

The ordinary questions sometimes help us get further along toward seeing the object for what it is. About a Broadway adaptation such as Tad Mosel's of James Agee's *A Death in the Family,* for example, we can ask the conventional questions concerning drama, and we can come to see why the failures come where they do: in the dialogue, self-consciously sweet but impoverished; in the tone and the governing attitudes, determinedly wistful and sentimentalized egregiously beyond Agee's aims; in Mosel's attempt to wring a few inspiring "universals" out of what he has first conceived, apparently, as a nostalgic period-piece, with the result that what is communicated is happily beyond specification: a little soft brooding on the burdens life continues to inflict upon us and a certain disembodied wonder and pride that we manage somehow to bear them.

Going further, we can, if we choose, take into account Mosel's obvious wish to do Agee's novel justice and ask: Why does it happen with so unhappy a frequency that what begins in reverence and generous feelings ends up full of the most obviously sentimental gambits, of a strained cuteness (Mosel's handling of the children), and heavy-handed efforts at "warm" comedy? We can deal, that is to say, with failures of craft that are inseparable from failures of feeling and attitude; and in the process we might easily move from novel to play to film. Or, on the other hand, we might take up the problem of the "soft stoicism" and the pseudo-poetic conception of stagecraft and human personality on which it rests, noting their combined effect on the statement the play uncomfortably both wants and does not want to make.

In any case, after we have finished with such analysis, should we still crave a metaphysics—one necessarily involved in invidious quibbling over the key terms in the cultural debate; in the high statesmanship of "cultural democracy"; one that brings us to various seizures of guilt and snobbery when we come face to face with ourselves and gives us the inordinate wish somehow to get everything larded with theory (sociological, psychoanalytical, of the most modish sort), mountain upon mountain; then we shall have to remain inordinately muddled —or hope instead for sober historical studies that will get us off the hook of our heavily committed moralizing. On the other hand, if we are able to do without metaphysics, the troublesome ordering abstractions that are often merely the sign of our pathos, then we shall have to take our objects where we find them, say what needs saying as we apply whatever modes of analysis suit them best, and teach others to use them. The only integration, after all, of "mass" and "elite" will occur within the experience of our attending well to the whole range of communication. It is too late for Utopia; we can no longer believe in the possibility of the unified American community. And we cannot go on forever looking for the appearance of the Apocalypse in the offerings of mass entertainment and the mass media. Loose historical generalization combined with pseudo-aristocratic criticism of mass culture leads only to unloosed fantasies of ruin and degradation, although certainly there is a good deal of soft degradation around—the nicely bearable kind—to inspire the fantasies.

III

I wish to deal now with issues that cannot be resolved easily, nor even be put properly within the limits of a single essay, but which I think ought to be at least somewhere in the backs of our minds when we consider the possibilities of television. I must designate my subject merely as attitudes toward art and the uses of art, and in connection with it I want to examine in an admittedly overly schematic way the work of James Agee. The work taken as a whole, schematically, is interesting for our purposes on account of the absolutely serious way in which Agee regarded popular culture and the perfect earnestness of his commitment to the camera as the great maker of twentieth century sensibility. Studies of writers whose work makes the easy generalizations about culture (mass or elite) hard to come by may help us to develop modes of critical analysis; they enable us to appreciate both the special possibilities and the problems of the newer media; and, perhaps even more important, they can save us from indulging too far the somewhat mistaken emphasis on improving TV that is so preponderantly a feature of public discourse concerning the mass media. We must conceive of the possibilities of TV at the same time that we observe how writers conceive of the responsibilities of art. And here it is especially useful, I think, to follow the leads offered by a writer who was himself a critic of popular culture.

It is easy to feel about James Agee that although he wanted desperately "to be a writer," he set little store by the achievement of an orderly *oeuvre* of serious writing, or by what he took, I think, to be the dangerous fetishism of art. There was not simply the refusal, apparently, to be recruited by the avant-garde, to find a high safe niche within the pages of *Partisan Review*; there was a good deal of nasty, somewhat unfocused belligerence, an overbothering with the clerisy of modern writing, whom he took to be rather overworried by their fate. Indeed, it is clear, in retrospect, that Agee was fighting against two cultural styles that he found threatening: that of the avant-garde, with its specialized techniques for dealing with the specialized difficulties of modern life, and that of Luce journalism with its impersonal documentary techniques and its displays of empty fireworks, not to speak of what Marshall McLuhan calls its "psychopathology." Possibly Agee was unfair to the avant-garde, but he was annoyed by its self-conscious proprietorship over modern literature and what he took to be its extravagant seriousness about its American fate, by not so much the political obviousness of *Partisan Review* as by its small, intramural leftism, by a tepid, strangely academic solemnity—by the incapacity of its writers to be as simply devout before the magnificently variegated world as he was himself.

One does not know what problems he met when, in the late forties, he went to Hollywood; in any case, these can easily be guessed; we are overly familiar with them from other sources. What is important for us, I believe, is not to pick out the minor and perhaps too obvious excellences of the screenplays—*The African Queen*, *The Bride Comes to Yellow Sky*, and *Noa Noa* (based on the life of Gauguin), among them—but rather to see the career that Agee made for himself, strange and shapeless as it was, as giving utterance to attitudes toward art which he not only never betrayed, but lived by, and about which he meditated over and over again in the letters to Father Flye. These attitudes grow out of the exacerbating experience of writing *Let Us Now Praise Famous Men* (Boston: Houghton Mifflin Co., 1941). At first they have to do with the problems Agee faced in finding himself a human being in the world: with discovering how one could justly know, honor, celebrate; how one could make the process of knowing itself an act of celebrating the things which surround one, in whose life one participates because one is surrounded and must attune one's existence to them. In *Let Us Now Praise Famous Men*, the process of knowing does not end in one's becoming habituated to ordinary things, in one's taking them as merely the fine raw data of experience. Instead, Agee attempts to record something of the inexhaustible particularity of ordinary things, not so much to make them new as to bear witness to how it is possible to see them newly, lovingly, as one surrenders to them.

So we see Agee in *Let Us Now Praise Famous Men* again and again exalting "the real," the simple, irreducible realities with which he was surrounded, and making the infinitely delicate attention to things a kind of moral duty, a spiritual obligation. Indeed, the aesthetic ideal that emerges out of Agee's cele-

bration of the magnificent otherness of life, informs all the work
he produced after the initial (and only) volume of poems, *Permit Me Voyage* (New Haven: Yale University Press, 1934),
and most centrally the film criticism. More important, Agee's
commitment to this ideal almost forced him to concern himself
with popular culture. By placing so heavy an emphasis on the
worth of unmediated reality, Agee came to consider the possibilities of film as an art that could serve to break down the
separation between the popular and elite.

Obviously Agee was far from being a naive propagandist in
behalf of "realistic" art. He wished to see dignity bestowed
upon the actual, not to have the actual reduced to the size of
art; and what he valued so highly was the world *before* art
could transform it, before the original and enduring particularity of things is absorbed by the reason, the will, of art. So
there is no need to worry about a "reductive realism" here, a
slicing away, a niggardly and comfortable realism. The fact is
that one always feels in Agee a magnificent Christian piety before the real world, a piety that is perfectly spontaneous and
that leads him to a joyful apprehension and acceptance of
things in their minute particularity. The ideal by which Agee
lived was that of direct, of adequate response to what exists
apart from us in its imposing otherness; what he experienced
at moments of direct and adequate response was the Words-
worthian joy that arises out of the hospitality of the self to the
world: a joy that rewards devout attention and willing surrender. *Let Us Now Praise Famous Men* records Agee's struggle
to find a form in which to represent his sense of "the dignity of
actuality"—the real world restored, as it were, not transformed;
known so deeply, indeed, that it would be beyond transform-
ing. This struggle is witnessed over and over again in the book,
and it is in working through the struggle, in loving all the
problematic otherness of the world that gives one the need to
struggle, that Agee moves toward the rapt visionary pages of
pure meditation: those pages that force us to think of *Let Us
Now Praise Famous Men* as a prose poem whose end is to celebrate, to sanctify, whatever surrounds us in the world—what-

ever needs no surrogate and must be affirmed against all of
its conceivable surrogates.

It is possible to view the struggle as of very mixed value,
needlessly exacerbated, appallingly self-conscious, its aesthetic
thoroughly muddled, its morality dubiously romantic, the product of an unexamined sentimental anarchism. But it is more to
the point to notice something crucial to Agee's entire outlook:
that for him ordinary reality was literally miraculous, hardly
something that was good to get into art in nicely measured
doses, and that as early as 1936 he had begun to search for contemporary forms in which some part of the miracle could be
represented. As he began to search, he found himself opposing
certain views of the resources and uses of art, and the attitudes
toward human beings that they fostered. The opposition to Luce
journalism was rather easy, of course; Agee had served a
strangely serious apprenticeship. More interesting, I imagine,
was his fretting, often belligerent, sometimes despairing consciousness of the burden of language, as he had begun to think
of it: all too mediating, discursive, impersonal; casting a shadow across the radiant consciousness of the world he wanted so
much to experience in his own life. Viewed as a series of medi-
tations on the possibility of such consciousness of the world,
Let Us Now Praise Famous Men is about the most agonizing of
questions: about how the writer possessed by a sense of the
immense "dignity of actuality" can hold to a bare minimum
the necessary sacrifice of the real world to the imperious demands of form—can allow things in themselves to manifest
their abounding grace. It was as though Agee, driven as he was
to honor again and again "the dignity of actuality," was pro-
testing against the triumph of modernism in the arts: against,
say, the apparently boundless power to transform reality witnessed in the highest manifestations of literary art in the twentieth century. He was, as it were, an anti-mythic writer, since
he wanted to live without myth, without "the absurd," without
the comforting conceptual props of the political left, so to absorb, as much as this is possible in art, the full phenomenal
power of what is: "the cruel radiance of what is." A properly

suggestive gloss is contained in the next to the last stanza of
Wallace Stevens' poem, "Sunday Morning."

> Supple and turbulent, a ring of men
> Shall chant in orgy on a summer morn
> Their boisterous devotion to the sun,
> Not as a god, but as a god might be,
> Naked among them, like a savage source.[6]

Agee, needless to say, was far from a "primitive," although
it is easy enough to imagine him celebrating a "boisterous devotion to the sun," since he felt very strongly the need for self-
surrendering devotion, for worship of the "savage source" as
the source, in fact, of joy. It is important to note, then, that
Agee's intention was at the farthest extreme from those who
wish to reduce the novel to a value-free form of detailed notation, in the current fashion of some French novelists like Alain
Robbe-Grillet. In any case, Agee would have considered, I suspect, that the aesthetic of the anti-novel, taken literally as a
way of coming to terms with life, is only another mode of escape from the real world, an escape made good, if at all, by
one's perversely refusing to see it as anything more than a body
of randomly constituent fact. One does not celebrate the "savage source" of life, the reality principle, by being frightened
of it.

To sum up: Agee had begun by attempting, in *Permit Me
Voyage* (1934), to write in traditional forms, in the formal sonnet and epithalamium, for example. For whatever reasons (and
the reasons can be guessed at), except for a number of fugitive
poems, he gave up the attempt early in his career. Under the
influence of his childhood fascination with film and the powerful feeling he had come to have for "the real," he then became
increasingly concerned with discovering a form (or, in the jar-
gon of our day, an anti-form) that would allow him to express
his great intuitive sympathy for whatever is offered in experi-

---

[6] Wallace Stevens, *Collected Poems* (New York: Alfred A. Knopf, Inc.,
1954), pp. 69-70.

ence that defies or awes or simply affronts the creative imagination, the rage for order. The religious-rhapsodic consciousness of *Let Us Now Praise Famous Men* which had charged itself with the obligation of utter faithfulness to an experience at
once gravely personal and exquisitely ceremonial, and bitterly
incomplete, bitterly inadequate, is disciplined out of existence,
so to speak, in *A Death in the Family* (New York: Ivan Obo-
lensky, Inc., 1957). The "cruel radiance of what is" that Agee
had exalted in *Let Us Now Praise Famous Men* is no longer the
subject of a series of more or less unstructured approaches to
matter-of-fact notation, on the one hand, and to visionary prose
poems, on the other. The distinction between the two kinds of
representation collapses; fact and vision become concentrated
in the flow of experience, person to person. The result is an
exemplary popular novel, one in which the strained nostalgia
of so much in popular culture is held in check by a language
that steadfastly refuses to devour its subject: the articulation
of sacred gesture within the small vulnerable routine of family
life, as this is observed both from within and without, in its
happy moments of right feeling and in its violent disruption.

It would be easy to set the "poetic realism" that Agee was so
much committed to against the rather timid, lachrymose, dis-
turbingly intramural realism I have touched on in speaking of
Rod Serling's *Requiem for a Heavyweight*. And to a certain
extent the comparison could prove instructive. It could help
bring out attitudes from which grow responsibilities. What
Emerson designated as "the near, the low, the common" was
for Agee simply not available to being fit nicely into the received conventions of art. In fact, it was characteristic of Agee
that he was fearful of the devouring energy of art, that he
thought of art as entailing too ready a sacrifice of what he
counted precious in experience. Hence there was always a tension between his need to impose a ceremonial order on reality
and a conflicting need to approach as near as possible the dis-
crete and irreducible pieces of reality he wanted to honor—to

which he wanted literally to bear witness. There is little tension in Serling's attitudes toward the making of art, let alone of popular culture, and little informed awareness of the responsibilities of the maker to the real world. For Serling, the real world yields easily to the received conventions. If not, there are always the Max Baers and the Maxie Rosenblooms around to obviate the need for invention, the real pugs in an unreal world.

It is our task, I think, to popularize other attitudes, and of course this is a hard task, perhaps (more so than we might like it) one necessarily involved in moralizing of the kind we find in Agee's generously humane film criticism. We may not always be sure where the moralizing is to take us and our students, but this will be surely beyond the just appreciation of examples of popular culture. We can begin with the interpretation of texts, moving from here to the interpretation of ourselves, our world, as we and it are represented in the texts. Perhaps we can show something of the difficulty and complexity of the transaction of art with the real world, focusing in the process on works that seem transparently unworried by any of the difficulties and uninformed by any part of the enabling tension the difficulties inspire; hence from Rod Serling to James Agee. Or we can choose less strikingly contrasted cases. Explication nowadays is nothing if not a moral enterprise, and we are stuck, I think, with the moralizing, now an ordinary dimension of literary study in our time, entailed by its special needs.

When we look back on the vision projected by Emerson and Whitman, it must strike us as somewhat preposterous, incapable of fulfillment in live works. Both Emerson and Whitman were concerned, inevitably, with "the spirit of the place," with country-making, the achievement of a national identity; and we are now a country made. We have established our identity in numerous ways, not the least of all through our literature, if not through the Utopian activity of a "divine literatus"; but the record does not offer evidence of some grandiose, overreaching American identity at last achieved. We cannot take from it an American metaphysic, only a sense of process: a sense of the possibilities of American speech and "the spirit of the place." As we well know, Emerson and Whitman were given to prophecy; they envisaged not only a literature that would place "the near, the low, the common" on the record, but the achieved American Primer, so to speak, and such are perhaps beyond the invention of poets—at least of poets who can no longer conceive the writing of American Epics. We cannot find ourselves now by at last establishing our Primer; we have pioneered too far, have created too much. The great American facts that the poet was to name, and in naming, sanctify, are scarcely as available to the imagination nowadays as they were in Emerson's day. Indeed, the inspirationalism of Emerson and Whitman appears to be a nineteenth century style, now lost to us. But of course we continue to examine the transaction into which art enters with the ordinary world—one that grows increasingly less real for us, that administers somewhat less generously than Emerson hoped to our need of Spirit, or simply of meaning; and during a time of manifest disbelief in "ordinary reality" except as it lends itself to parody or to the strenuously manic comedy that is fast becoming the dominant mode of the novel of the sixties.

What we see, I have argued, is how difficult it is to treat everyday reality honorably, responsibly, without false puffing-up and false filling-in. Serling gives us the occasion not to promulgate a theory of popular culture or to examine the prophecies of the past, but rather to make *ad hoc* discriminations as we move from the television play, tough-minded and full of moments of wild beauty, to its metamorphosis in the movie adaptation. Such analysis, somewhat more developed, might be extended to include the Broadway plays of Chayefsky, for example. It would be a good exercise to trace the honest sentimentality of *Marty* through the other plays, *The Middle of the Night* (a television play, Broadway play, and movie), *The Tenth Man*, and *Gideon*. There are interesting failures along the way. One can ask: Are these to be explained as a consequence of a popular artist's attempt to puff up his art so that it expands hopefully into "philosophy," full of the simple wisdom of the sages? Or is it that Chayefsky could not help but learn to say too much, as in the rather dull *The Middle of the Night*, not being able to withstand the common pressure to put in a good word for love? Perhaps the putatively popular writer is defenseless against the machinery of a culture-hungry society, inevitably coming to have an exaggerated and harmful respect for serious art, the nature of which he is likely to misconceive. The real seriousness of Chayefsky, of course, is in the small epiphany of *Marty*, not in the homily on love at the end of *The Middle of the Night*, nor in the elusive and ill-handled myths of *The Tenth Man* and *Gideon*. Chayefsky appears to be the victim of a well-known disease: the Broadway eclecticism that compels him to seek to know more than it is good for him to know, so that he moves from a small piece of reality honestly rendered to the faraway and difficult, to religious exaltation and agony, to *kitsch* exotic. The analyst of popular culture must inquire, ultimately, into the "natural history" of so palpable a misreading of one's gifts, rather than nostalgically mourn the end of the Golden Age of Television Drama—a Golden Age that it is possible to overvalue, which certainly could stand some hard analysis, and which is, as we read the past nowadays, far behind us.

Richard J. Stonesifer

Ethos by Esso:
In What America? and
Culture in Transition
from Esso World Theatre,
February and May, 1964

An English voice intoned at one point in the BBC's documentary *Television and the World* that "10 percent of American
TV is good, 5 percent is superb." The percentages are arbitrary,
of course, and not worth quibbling over. But what is evident
to any critic is that American television in its current phase is
very much like the little girl in the nursery rhyme—when it
is good, it is very, very good; and when it is bad, it is horrid. The
BBC attempt to explore both the impact and the quality of television programing in such places as Italy, Thailand, Egypt, Japan, and the United States went on to add that the major documentaries produced in the U.S. usually end up worthy of being
placed in the American top 5 percent, but that most of the rest
of American programing gives "a peculiar image of the West."
It is a judgment with which it would be hard to quarrel.

The BBC assessment preceded by some months the announcement on October 17, 1963, that Esso would finance a new
American television venture, the *Esso World Theatre*.

My own guess is that the bulk of the Esso series may belong
comfortably within the "good" 10 percent, with some parts of

it poking into the "superb" 5. Why all of it does not merit standing within the top 5 percent is some of our concern here.

If nothing else, the series provides some patterns worth pondering. On the whole, the Esso experiment has been a noble one, and it might be hoped that we can have more of the same. Someone at Esso either had a sound idea or was sold one, and in either case nothing but praise can go to a corporation with conscience sufficiently large to embroil itself with cultural concerns. In doing so, Esso has joined the ranks of the corporations that perceptive Americans should salute—Hallmark, U.S. Steel, Xerox, Firestone—which have been willing to finance television programing for minority tastes and then to stand back and to allow creativity, experimentation, and even occasional artistic wrongheadedness control what finally emerges. If there are things wrong with the *Esso World Theatre* (and there are), Esso nevertheless did its part. And it did it with an unselfishness and a sophistication that is so rare among sponsors as to be regarded as wonderful in the usually corrosive world of commercial television, a world which *Show* magazine described (in the same October in which the *World Theatre* series was announced) as "the least grateful, most abrasive, exhausting, moneygrubbing, coldblooded showplace the world of entertainment has ever known."

Esso did not go into the *World Theatre* venture blindly. A corporation that had already financed *The Festival of the Performing Arts*, it had also made *The Age of Kings* available to American audiences and had been responsible for saving *The Play of the Week* from immediate cancellation back in 1960 when New York's WNTA-TV announced that it had discovered that quality drama on television was unlikely to pay for itself. It had long aligned itself on the side of whatever angels guard cultural concerns, and for its part in these three acts of cultural charity, it had received something over 50,000 letters from grateful viewers. Unlike the networks (where a mere 50,000 leters are quickly calibrated to equal less than two tenths of one of Mr. Nielsen's celebrated and all-important rating points), it had been impressed with this outpouring of viewers' sentiment in favor of quality programing. Esso knew, and it proved to be prophetically correct, that the *World Theatre* might well elicit less audience response than the previous ventures. But it went ahead, confident that a corporation of its magnitude can do itself no harm, and might do itself great good, by splitting the levels of its sponsorship of programing, assuming that those who love literature and art as well as those in the popcorn set are likely to meet at the gasoline pump (putting tigers in their tanks!).

The prospectus on the *World Theatre* announced that eight programs would be presented, at one month intervals extending from January through May and resuming in September through November of 1964. Initial telecasting was to be confined to commercial stations in New York, Washington, Baltimore, Boston, New Haven, Rochester, and Richmond, though arrangements were later made to air the series over an ETV outlet in Philadelphia where no commercial station would provide time away from the nurses with their bedpans and the cowboys with their sixshooters for it. Each program was to deal with a separate country—England, Nigeria, Japan, Greece, U.S.A., India, Sweden, France—and each was to reflect that nation's "national heritage in literature and the performing arts." Each was to be largely filmed in the nation involved and to utilize the best talent of that country available for it. Each was to be "an anthology in which the selections were to illustrate a theme characteristic of the national culture." Drama, music, poetry, dance, literary excerpts, commentary, all these were available to be interwoven in each. The programs were not to be travelogues and not really to be documentaries in the usual sense of that word, but were rather to be real explorations into national character. Bert Lawrence, a New York film producer, was named producer, and production started in Delphi on the Greek segment in mid-October 1963, with Robert Graves serving as host-narrator.

Aware that no single program could possibly catch the sweep of a complex nation's entire cultural heritage, the producers singled out tightly circumscribed themes where possible. Thus,

England was to be dealt with in terms of the omnipresent
Puritan and Cavalier strains in its character; Japan in terms
of the significance which discipline, pattern, and form have on
its artistic conceptions and creations; Greece was to be handled
with excerpts from Euripides, Sophocles, and Aeschylus significant in their insight into moral law, assumed to be a salient
characteristic of the ancient Greek heritage; India with a
potpourri of items from its long cultural history; Sweden with
a ballet from Strindberg's *Miss Julia* and excerpts from Dag
Hammerskjöld's Diary; France by treating three aspects of
love.

If all of these are obvious choices, only the last would seem
to be a concession to popular American expectations, and even
here no one can find fault with a format that covers *Cyrano
de Bergerac* and Moliere's *The Would-Be Gentleman*, with the
Folies Bergere nowhere in evidence. All of the programs are
eminently worth watching, and two of them, the hour devoted
to Nigeria and the program spent in dissecting the U.S.A.,
offer a study in contrasts, both in content and methodology,
that is certainly worthwhile. Indeed, the initial screening of
the Nigerian hour, in February of 1964, provided the first evidence that something unusual might be emerging and that
those interested in television program design ought to pay
attention.

All of this, or much of it at any rate, has no apparent bearing
on a critical assessment of the individual programs, particularly if one chooses to adopt the strict stance of an electronic
New Critic, evaluating each as an independent and quite
separate work of television art, ignoring its genesis and insisting that nothing matters but the finished work itself. The sad
fact is, however, that, given the current state of television, such
a stance is unrealistic. A finished television program is the
result of a series of accommodations and compromises. Programs on any level—horrid through superb—do not arrive
before us by some sort of electronic immaculate birth, sprung
like Venus full-blown from the swirling seas. One can't really
settle back before the flickering screen to play critic precisely

as one might before a new poem by the likes of Richard Eberhart or Stanley Kunitz, exhibited pristine upon the newly
printed page, the product of one mind's gropings and compromises with itself and accommodations made only to language's
flexibility or rigidity. The commercial underpinnings of the
cultural concerns have never been more evident in any artistic
field than they are in television, for one thing, and one consequently ought to delve into *how* a program comes into being,
why, and *what went on* to sully its purity or to improve its
format as it moved from conception to screening if one wishes
to analyze fully and to understand thoroughly. And if this is
an essential stance for the critic after the program's production,
it calls for an increase in a similar process before production.
One wishes, and pretty violently, that more television decision-
makers would develop what I will call the Goethe-habit, asking
themselves his essential three questions in a somewhat new
form—What is intended artistically and thematically? Are we
bringing it off satisfactorily? Is it worth doing? This might raise
the nervous breakdown rate along Madison Avenue, but its
impact on programing might be revolutionary.

II

Against a background of throbbing music, we hear a voice
and we see a house built of mud for the expressed purpose of
being washed to nothingness by the inevitable storms. "Not
the product, not the final artifact but the act of creation," says
the voice going on to explain that we are looking at an Mbari
house in eastern Nigeria, erected in honor of Ala, goddess of
earth and creation. The voice is that of Nigerian playwright
Wole Soyinka, who goes on to explain that Ala is the most
revered goddess among the Ibo people and that the practice
of building in her honor mud shrines which disintegrate under
the force of nature to necessitate the building of new shrines,
all in an endless cycle, "is an activity of communion which may
last two months to a year." The camera moves over figures
adorning the mud house, with the music softened to that of an

Ibo harp, as Soyinka ties what we have just seen visually to
the keystone of all that is to follow:

> Continuity is preserved by the absorption of experience, trivial or
> profound, for an artist's sincerity comes, not from solemnity, but
> from a true response to experience. Tradition for the Ibo artist is
> not stagnation but a regenerative consciousness of life in all its
> varied manifestations. Tradition is *now*, and is born of every ex-
> perience, not buried in the stillness of antiquity. This freedom is
> the true legacy of the modern African, the freedom to reshape, to
> select and to reject, to build new images around the forms of the
> past, to reinterpret the ancient idioms through the uniqueness of
> a personal, contemporary experience. For the new African, form
> is a movement which constantly supersedes itself.

And then, as the camera follows Soyinka retreating into the
distance of a village street, a voice recites a poem ("Water-
maid" by Okigbe), two lines of which reiterate sharply the
mutability theme that has been struck:

> So brief her presence—
> so brief with mirrors around me.

This is the opening sequence in *Nigeria: Culture in Transition*. One ought to watch it conscious of Max Lerner's statement
early in his *America as a Civilization* (New York: Simon and
Schuster, 1957-1961) that "the versions a culture has of its own
strength and success are as important parts of its tradition as
the versions it has of its origins or mission." One ought to
watch aware too that somehow Soyinka standing in the street
of a Nigerian village has linked hands with Emerson, who in
his time also saw the advent of "a new race, a new religion, a
new state, a new literature." And one does watch this opening
sequence with a special wry irony if one knows what preceded
it in the creation of this particular program.

An American television producer, anxious to present an
hour about Nigeria, easily falls into the trap. Holed up somewhere amidst the cacophony of New York, he sketches out a
script embodying the content he wishes to include. Bert

Lawrence did precisely this, and took it to Soyinka, who re-
acted with laudable asperity, vowing that he would have no
part of the project, reiterating a position which he had trumpeted at the Edinburgh Film Festival some months earlier:
"All you want from Africa is bare bosoms, freaks, and all sorts
of exotica. All you want is what Hollywood and what Tarzan
films have been churning out for years! Let us," said Soyinka,
"find something meaningful for today." And so Lawrence gave
Soyinka the reins, exhibiting either a high pragmatic sense or
consummate wisdom, or both.

There are no bare bosoms and little that is freakish in *Culture in Transition* as a result. What there is instead is an
almost superbly tailored amalgam of contemporary Nigerian
literature and art to illustrate how its writers and artists are
taking from the past to create the cultural future. And what
follows in the remainder of the hour offers evidence aplenty
that the Africa of Conrad's *Heart of Darkness* ought finally to
be relegated exclusively to the province of the late-late movie
on television, and that the educated African writer can hold
his own in sophistication and intelligence with his peers anywhere.

We are moved to accept this revelation by a series of contrasts, the first of which immediately follows the sequence
recounted above. In Africa the dance is the highest form of
art, the chief method of portraying and giving vent to the
emotions, though Soyinka in his commentary observes that
poetry thoroughly permeates the life of the people. The scene
suddenly shifts to some Agbor Dancers performing before the
Obi (King) of Agbor and a joyous crowd. Now the typical
assumption of the Westerner is that African dancing is un-
mitigatedly sexual, savage, and even sinister, an assumption
based on what one dance critic once called "Uncle Tom-
Tomism." At first glance, what comes to the screen seems to
fit this—a man and a woman face each other, separated by a
distance of several feet, and the camera moves in to record
their dance, a dance replete with strong, thrusting pelvic
movements, bent knees and a swayed-back posture that is

nothing if not sex-seeming to the Western observer. It is a
dance that teems with an eroticism that could never find place
on an Ed Sullivan show were a Barrie Chase or a Juliet
Prowse the dancer. But then, with the camera alternating between shots of the dancers and the audience, a difference is
observed, a difference which takes these "bumps and grinds"
light-years away from their counterparts delivered amidst
the smoky gloom of a nightclub runway, a milieu which seldom promotes thoughts about the Earth Mother.

For that is what we are watching, a point made clear when
we shift the focus of our attention slightly from what we are
seeing to what we are also hearing from the voice-over—a poem
by John Pepper Clark:

> See her caught in the throb of a drum
> Tippling from hide-brimmed stem
> Down lineal veins to ancestral core
> Opening out in her supple tan
> Limbs like fresh foliage in the sun.

The camera catches pelvic thrusts, then to laughing audience,
to families healthily participating in a sensuality that is one
of the eternal verities, to the "King" of Obi (who wears
Western-style rimless glasses and a tribal robe!). This "King"
is not Kurtz, reveling of an evening. The joke, if one might
call it that, is on the Westerner, a point made clear as the voice-
over goes on:

> In trance she treads the intricate
> Pattern rippling crest after crest
> To meet the green clouds of the forest

ending with:

> Could I, early sequestered from my tribe,
> Free a lead-tethered scribe
> I should answer her communal call
> Lose myself in her warm caress
> Intervolving earth, sky and flesh.

D. H. Lawrence, in short, could not have done it better. And we have it here, on several hundred feet of film.

The sequence establishes the mood and format we are to move in henceforth. The program's content is never to stray far from man's essential attachment to the soil and the transitoriness of man's inevitable experience while he strides the earth, with constant alternation between the wholly modern and the ancient archetype. There is also a continued archness —and even a note of condescension here and there—on the part of the Nigerian spokesman facing the Western audience. The frenzied dance completed, for example, Soyinka comes on to tell us that "art is also served by popular interpreters, fulfilling creative functional needs." And then as we look at some examples, he adds that "panels from the untrained hands of this blacksmith now hang from the walls of modern commercial buildings. Pop Art, to use the favorite term, flourishes in every streetcorner and private workshop."

From this we swing to a group of comic masqueraders, then to a sequence on talking drums (with a poem paying tribute to Ogun, Master of Strategy, addressed significantly for those with anthropological interests as "Ogun is dual, Ogun is seven"); then to the front porch of a Nigerian home where a skillful Nigerian actor, Segun Olusola, reads a charming excerpt from Amos Tutuola's *The Palm-Wine Drinkard* (London: Faber and Faber, 1952) that puts us as close to Chaucer and to the medieval fabliaux as one is likely to get seated on the stoop of a Nigerian home; then to a sequence in which we see a group perform a bit from a Yoruba Folk Opera, a modern form of popular theater which reinterprets the ancient legends for modern audiences.

This last is not successful, resembling nothing so much as an extremely amateurish school play or camp skit, which it assuredly is not. But the technique involved is totally foreign to the Western observer, and the language barrier throws up obstacles that are not transcended by feeble attempts to make the spectacle meaningful. The few minutes consumed nevertheless raise the specter of virtually carefree intercontinental entertainment programing in a TelStar-dominated world in which ways must be found to bridge the gaps which language and cultural heritages create if we are not to remain necessarily indifferent to much that is central to many foreign cultures.

As if to compensate for thrusting us so unceremoniously into a thoroughly alien world, the producers of *Culture in Transition* snap us back with what might be regarded even as overcompensation, taking us not to some more comprehensible sector of activity in Nigeria but to two Negro Off-Broadway actors sequestered in a New York studio, each seated on a tall kitchen stool, who alternate in recitations of some modern Nigerian poetry. The two, Vinie Burrows and Earle Hyman, are excellent, and the poems they read—by John Pepper Clark, Gabriel Okara, Michael Echerue, and Christopher Okigbe—are astringent, evocative lyrics, each a *cri de coeur* composing a whole that does not need to be comprehended in its entirety to be appreciated. Only phrases really stick to one's mind as the four poems are read, for they have the cryptic quality of much modern English poetry—"arched like a boa bent to kill," "between the oyster-beach and the greens . . . sere and barren coast," "yet in my father's house I cannot sleep," ". . . out of a violated past," ". . . Singed Hair and Dark Skin," or most memorably:

> For does not the Holy Writ
> Loud peddled abroad
> To approve imperial flaws and fraud
> Does it not say true:
> "Knock and it shall be opened unto you"?

And it was probably wise to get actors with American-oriented voices to read them, for Nigerian-oriented English poses some difficulties for the American, a fact which is evident at a few points in the recitation of the excerpt from *The Palm-Wine Drinkard* where clipped words are lost on the sound track.

What follows is a longish excerpt from Soyinka's *The Strong Breed*, played out for us on the streets of Pjokodo in western Nigeria and serving as the climax of the hour. It runs twenty-five minutes, uninterrupted, and is acted by members of the 1960 Masks Theatre Group of Ibadan, probably the leading theatrical group in Nigeria. Its anthropological significance is great, its dramatic value considerable. And it provides a memorable capstone for the program. But what is most important about it is that at one and the same time it serves to illustrate the way in which the contemporary Nigerian writer is using ancient material as modern material, and that the bridge between the emerging African nations and the West, culturally at least, may not be as long a one—or as difficult to construct—as some have imagined. For *The Strong Breed* has ties with the Christ story, with the ancient scapegoat idea, with all purification ceremonials. It resembles nothing so much as Shirley Jackson's "The Lottery" from contemporary American literature, though if one desires to establish even further connections one might do so with Nathaniel West's *Miss Lonelyhearts*, perhaps a bit fancifully. But Soyinka has pointed out that his play is essentially about "man's need to sacrifice himself for man."

The scene is a Nigerian village, and the time is New Year's Day. The principal characters are Eman, the village teacher and a stranger to this area, and his assistant Sunma, the daughter of one of the leaders of the village. The two are considering leaving the village, but Eman cannot bring himself to leave, much to Sunma's dismay. It is the tradition in the village, going back to time immemorial, as a way of marking the New Year to select a member of the tribe as a sacrifice, ceremonially loading on to him the sins and burdens of the group and banishing him, driving him off into the surrounding jungles to certain death. A weakling, a deformed and crippled one, a man who is assumed to be of no value, is customarily seized for the purpose; indeed, the villagers give refuge to such occasionally in order to have them available for the sacrificial purpose, thus removing the necessity of a member of their own group assuming the role. At the moment there is one such in the village, a ten-year-old idiot named Ifada, befriended by Eman. He has been marked for this purpose, a fact which Sunma seems aware of but which Eman has not realized.

Eman is a man who enjoys being alone and being different. There is, he says, "peace in being a stranger." But Sunma knows that in this village there is also danger in being a stranger, and she knows Eman thoroughly—knows his aloofness but also his incapacity to hold himself away from such as Ifada. "Those who have much to give fulfill themselves in total loneliness," he tells her at one point, to which she answers "Then there is no love in what you do," and he responds by telling her: "There is. Love comes to me more easily with strangers. I know that I find consummation only when I have spent myself for an absolute stranger."

Ifada is seized to serve as the village's "carrier," the one to be sacrificed. He escapes and seeks sanctuary with Eman and is discovered. When Eman attempts to dissuade the villagers from their purpose, he is told that, as a stranger, he can volunteer himself as a replacement. He does this, is driven from the village, and because he has not comported himself in the manner deemed fitting for a carrier (the chosen one is drugged into joyousness about his fate, a procedure which Eman refuses), he is pursued into the jungle and killed.

Soyinka's play is a work of considerable subtlety, with character delineations of some complexity, and a mere outline of it cannot convey its value—anymore than a comparable outline of Hawthorne's "Young Goodman Brown," for instance, would do. What it is also is a dramatic work of a kind seldom seen on television, one whose reverberations last far longer than the dying out of the tiny pinpoint of light that quavers and diminishes for a few seconds when the set is turned off.

III

In What America? contains as the largest section of its concluding part the poignant scene from Arthur Miller's *Death of a Salesman* in which Willy Loman's widow and sons stand beside his grave. It was an obvious choice for a program dedicated to the idea of revealing aspects of the United States, with its celebration of the American salesman, "a man way out there in the blue, riding on a smile and a shoeshine." As John Kenneth Galbraith once put it, "At *Death of a Salesman* everyone carried Willy Loman's huge suitcases for an evening." But its inclusions set up an ironic contrast with *Nigeria: Culture in Transition*. There also an excerpt from a play, as we have seen, serves as the program's climax. In each a man dies and in each case because of what we might call "the system." Willy Loman's widow, kneeling by his grave, says that he shouldn't have killed himself, that for the "first time in thirty-five years we were just about free and clear," and ends the scene semi-hysterically, crying as her sons lead her away that now "We're free and clear . . . We're free . . . We're free . . . We're free." She and Sunma are sisters under the skin, and Sunma's statement when Eman tells her that he will not leave the village applies equally to Loman's widow: ". . . this was to be a new beginning for us, and I placed my fate wholly in your hands."

Moreover, the Nigerian villagers, gazing aloft at the swinging body of Eman, have carried out the ritual assigned by tradition to them and are supposed now to be "free and clear" for a year because of it. As we leave them, however, we know that they are consumed by guilt, this man's death having been the death of part of them too, and their guilt our guilt, as much our guilt as that which we feel standing with Linda beside Willy's open grave. It is not the only captivating correspondence, as we shall see, between the two programs.

In What America? is not, however, the neatly chiseled entity that *Culture in Transition* is, and the reason goes, I think, far beyond the fact that those charged with its preparation must have approached their task virtually paralyzed by their realization that Hawthorne was probably right: "We have so much country that we really have no country at all."

There is no finely honed intelligence akin to that of Wole Soyinka in evidence, for one thing, dominating the material and insisting that all of it do service to one overriding consideration—the precise illustration of one clearly conceived and reasonable theme. The result was probably definitively expressed by Howard Thompson in the New York *Times* (Sunday, May 17, 1964) when he forecast the program on the eve of its appearance as "a literary, all-American apple pie with, to put it mildly, patchwork crust."

The program is set up as a three-act play, the intermissions fixed in what on first viewing seems to be a completely arbitrary way. Closer inspection gives the lie to this, however, for it would seem that Act I is supposed to differ somewhat from the emphasis achieved in Act II, and Act II is intended to differ equally from Act III. What the three acts together give us is an hour during which in thirty separate presentations, a few of them dovetailed neatly, a total of twenty-seven Americans speak to us, their words either recited by members of a cast headed by George C. Scott and his wife, Colleen Dewhurst, or presented in dramatized form—as, for example, are segments from *Babbitt*, a Phyllis McGinley poem, or a passage from Dos Passos about the adulation of James Dean. Dances, both in solo form and as mere background, interweave between some of the episodes or accompany them, and the musical background is predominantly one of jazz motifs.

The program opens on a Negro dancer, with a rear-projection of a semiabstract New York skyline in the background. Scott's voice intones Thomas Wolfe's words: ". . . it is a fabulous country; the only fabulous country, it is the one place where miracles not only happen, but where they happen all the time." Then Scott himself is seen, as narrator, and he delivers the theme-speech for the show:

> The problem of who we are and what we are and in what America we live has always been of acute concern to the American people. From the very beginning of our existence, we have been the most self-conscious people on earth.
>
> Americans take inordinate pride in what they have done and at the same time feel inordinate shame at what they have failed to do. In the imaginative literature of the nation, here truly is its image and reflection . . . the great paradox that is America.

This bit of warmed over and alarmingly truncated material that might have been written by someone who had read Eric Larrabee's *Self-Conscious Society* fleetingly but not well having been delivered, four actors and actresses standing in a line deliver—one line apiece—four assertions which lead a fifth, Joanna Miles, to intone a Carl Sandburg piece about l-o-v-e ("I'm asking, is love an elephant?"). A Negress steps forward and recites a bit from Whitman about grass; then a switch and a boy stretched flat upon what is presumed to be a raft looks skyward and, impersonating Huck Finn, discourses on how the stars were made. A danceline, led by George Scott, prances in, singsonging an old Shirley Temple ditty about her pet dog Corky, followed by Colleen Dewhurst (wearing a huge hat to make the identification explicit) reciting a few paragraphs of purple prose from Hedda Hopper about Shirley's infatuation at age fifteen with Jack Agar. This is followed by a segment in which two merrymakers seated on a ferry give us Edna St. Vincent Millay's little classic about going back-and-forth-all-night-long; then to an actor who delivers three paragraphs of a diatribe which H. L. Mencken once penned on the unhappiness of schoolboys; then to a dramatized piece of one of James Agee's letters to Father Flye as he contemplates the worth of being or not being; and finally to a reading of a passage from Dos Passos about the hipsters' adulation of James Dean, this done with a Negro "cat" in the background attired in a leather jacket, and duck-tail hairdo, doing a kind of pantomimic dance.

The eleven segments compose Act I, and it is necessary to look at them as a unit and to try to see a purpose, misguided as it may have been, in their being arranged thus and presented in such a semisurrealistic manner. Act I, I hazard a guess, is intended to comment on the life of the young in our society. And this was thought to be a way of tucking it all together neatly, or not so neatly, depending on how you like such things. The tipoff that youth is indeed to be regarded as its unifying principle is given to us fleetingly as the tail on the initial Thomas Wolf piece: "It is the place of the strong joy of our youth . . . the magic city, when we know the most fortunate life

on earth would certainly be ours, that we were twenty and
could never die."

The difficulty is that between this and the segments that
follow comes George C. Scott and the theme-statement, which
has nothing to do with youth. And the theme-statement is
followed by Sandburg's playful piece, presumably addressed
to a child—or the childish—and having as much really to do
with children in Zanzibar as it does with kids on Chicago's
State Street. And this is followed by the Walt Whitman piece,
in which a child says "What is the grass?" and Whitman answers, deifying the grass in essence, calling the grass itself "the
produced babe of the vegetation," an interesting poetic idea
but one as applicable to the playing fields of Eton as to the
fields close to his home in Camden. This is followed by a
semidramatization of Huck Finn stargazing, which is no more
specifically American than Galileo's was Italian, even though
Huck is supposed to be a symbol for all American boydom and
presumably an inevitable inclusion here.

It is not until we get to the prancing danceline and Shirley
Temple's little doggie, and to Colleen Dewhurst in Hedda Hopper's big hat, that any precise *American* impact begins, commentary, that is, on things distinctively American. It begins at
this point, however, with a vengeance:

> What Shirley wanted wasn't a foreign title or a glamour playboy
> or a millionaire social snob . . . . The fact that she was Shirley
> Temple, the world's most treasured Valentine in person, didn't
> warp her direct mind or honest heart. Jack Agar was the first and
> only true love of her life.
>
> He was a buck private when Shirley first looked up into his blue
> eyes . . . . He hadn't a famous name or too much money . . . but
> he did have the same solid American background that Shirley
> had, the same sincerity and sweetness (Yep, men have it too). . . .

And it swings along nicely through a beautifully executed
reading of Edna St. Vincent Millay's "Recuerdo" (the first
verse omitted, perhaps for reasons of time but also perhaps because in it the young lovers quite explicitly state that they have

lain "on a hilltop underneath the moon"), through the Mencken bit on schoolboys, through the James Agee piece on the love of life in the face of personal despair, and through the Dos Passos cerebrations on the "poor mixed-up kid," the "motherless, brotherless, sisterless lone wolf brat strayed from the pack," who starved for affection is in love with himself seen in the image of James Dean.

Act II has fourteen similar segments, centered—as I dope it out—on the satisfactions and dissatisfactions in American life, though the assumption stemming from the first act is that what is treated here must cover the citizenry in their maturity (or in what the deodorant people call "the vitality years"). We start off with Emerson foreseeing the developing American colossus; then switch to a boy pushing a loaded supermarket cart, zigzagging, chanting a poem by Allen Ginsberg on "Walt Whitman's odyssey"; then to a recitation of Thomas Wolfe's "I believe that we are lost here in America" passage; then to Colleen Dewhurst doing a brilliant reading of Auden's "The Unknown Citizen"; then to a piece by Mencken on the selection of Coolidge as President and the uttering of a one-line bit of Coolidge banality—"When more and more people are thrown out of work, unemployment results"; then to Louise Tanner's observations on the fascination of the heroes and heroines of the literature of the 1920's; to a Fitzgerald passage about loneliness in New York; to a bit by I. J. Kapstein about hero worship; to a segment in which George C. Scott ensconced in a rocking chair speaks as Harry Golden on the strength of his Jewish mother; to four paragraphs from a Bette Davis pronouncement about herself, the worthlessness of sex and the worth of work, and a declaration about the new woman; to an assertion by Porfiro Rubirosa that bachelordom may be preferable to marriage to an heiress; to an acted-out reading of a Phyllis McGinley poem on the plight of the suburbanite contemplating the horrors of the contemporary world; and finally to two dramatized scenes from *Babbitt*, the first dealing with the Babbitts at home, the second showing us George addressing the annual dinner of the Zenith Rotary Club.

Act III starts with the graveyard scene from *Death of a Salesman*, then switches to a Negress who delivers an excoriating piece by Mark Twain on the puny pretensions of man as a supposedly favorite creature of God, and then shifts to a close-up of George C. Scott, shawl around his shoulders, impersonating Samuel Sewall standing at his mother's graveside in 1701 and delivering a few obituary remarks. Obviously, these three segments must be taken as something of a unit. Each concentrates on death and human worth, two of them concern statements made at actual gravesites, and the Twain piece seems to imply that the conquering worm is a wise and wholesome creature indeed in comparison to man. It is obvious that the three acts have been constructed on a chronological basis—youth, maturity, old age, and death. And Act III, then, *must* center on the value of the human being, and presumably seen in precise *American* terms. The difficulty with this formulation about theme, however, is that only the Arthur Miller scene specifically deals with a manifestation of Americana. Mark Twain was understudying the likes of Voltaire when he penned the passage used, and George C. Scott (shawl-encumbered) can do little with the Sewall passage to convince us that hypocrisy practiced on New England's shores differs markedly from the same human disease when in evidence anywhere north or south of Suez. Again, the focus has been lost, if specifically American commentary is the intention, and lost pretty disastrously.

But Act III shifts a bit halfway through, the concluding three segments exhibiting a changed tone. The new theme is implied—it might be, to put a title on it, "There is so worth too." And while the two segments that follow still key to death and immortality, they do so positively. A statement from Jack London ("I would rather that my spark should burn out in a brilliant blaze than it should be stifled in dry rot"), followed by Scott's recitation of part of Faulkner's Nobel Prize acceptance speech, brings us to the close, which is a few lines from Archibald MacLeish, the three concluding lines certainly intended to take us back to the beginning of Act I, where

Wolfe's "It is a fabulous country" is presumed to be still ringing in our ears:

> America is neither a land nor a people.
> A word's shape it is, a wind's sweep—
> America is alone.[1]

The voyage between the beginning (with Wolfe) and the ending (with MacLeish) is far from a smooth one, and no casual television viewer could be expected to glimpse the purpose and seeming methodology in the three-act design that I have sketched. Which, of course, is the chief fault in it: it is simply too recondite for the purpose. In *In What America?* the narrator comes in to our ken only twice, the first time when he enters to give us the two paragraphs of the "theme" I have already cited, the second when he enters to identify the George Babbitt dramatizations that end Act II. It is simply not enough, if we are to see the design I think is intended. We need someone to take us by the hand a little more frequently. Like Dante, we need a guide who has been over the terrain before! The intention, obviously, was to eliminate narration and connections and to allow the writers' voices to reach us unaided. But it simply does not succeed.

Act I, in any event, is, as I have indicated, a mottled affair thematically, with no real focus generated until we reach Shirley Temple—all this, of course, *if* the title of the program, *In What America?*, is to have any significance. If it does not, if literally no design in the program is to be looked for, then Act I, Act II, and Act III constitute only a sort of anthology arrived at on a higgledy-piggledy basis that does not even fit well with one of the goals announced in the April 24, 1964, press release from Esso heralding the show. "*In What America?* will offer," that document said, "an incisive look at the United States through the eyes of this nation's greatest boosters and severest critics—its own writers." Rubirosa, Shirley Temple,

---

[1] Archibald MacLeish, "American Letter," *Collected Poems 1917-1952* (New York: Houghton Mifflin Company, 1952), p. 63.

and Bette Davis are hardly to be regarded as such, and much of
what we get falls far outside "an incisive look at the United
States." If we are looking at the United States, the three act
design based on age-spans in the citizenry doesn't make much
sense either. Act III *has* structure, whether intended or not,
in that three of its six episodes tie together in one direction,
and three in another (though two of those three continue the
emphasis of the prior triad!), but the last three episodes provide a sufficiently upbeat ending to satisfy anyone, be he super-
patriot, optimistic follower of Norman Vincent Peale, or simpleminded exponent of that amorphous thing called "the American
Way," eloquently adumbrated by Babbitt in his Rotary Club
speech at the end of Act II. But *that* can't be what was intended either, using writers like London, Faulkner, and Mac-
Leish, even by television producers who know that the greatest
of the commandments in the vast wasteland is that happy endings for happy people with happy problems ought to be provided. And a little contemplation of Act II proves it.

"The program," said the advance announcement covering *In
What America?*, "will delve into the paradox of the apparent
pride Americans take in what they have done and their inordinate shame at what they have failed to do." This is strikingly like the theme which I think I find through the chaos
of Act II. And somehow its fourteen segments have to be made
to cohere into some rational design if the production, or the
main and middle part of it, is not to be written off as a kind
of inspired chaos.

I'm afraid I have to announce that I think the fourteen
parts do so cohere, but that the final result is somehow
distressing, even frightening, if what we are looking for is
evidence that the program focuses on anything that really
matters very much about the U.S.A. And one needn't be a
Rotarian applauding Babbitt's superficialities that are trumpeted at the end to question whether or not America has gotten
a fair shake in Act II. It simply hasn't. Nor has the bulk of the
citizenry.

And it hasn't because whoever was responsible for assem-

bling the bits that compose the format either had no very clear
idea of what America really is or Americans are, or had a distorted view. The America *he* lives in, to revert to George C.
Scott's thematic statement, comes through pretty strongly,
however, and since an anthology is always a peculiarly personal thing, perhaps one cannot logically object—except when
a prior claim has been made (as was clearly done in this case)
that we are to see all aspects of America exhibited. We start
by being told that America is a fabulous country. We ought
then to be in a position to object, and pretty vigorously, when
little that is fabulous about it is displayed, and when what is
displayed is largely a series of cynical and peripheral comments.

Obviously, one should not take press releases distributed
before programs are released as definitively stating their
themes. And particularly not this program, for I have been
told since its production that several scripts were written, discarded, pulled out, patched up, and that finally—in a kind of
desperation—the script that was seen in production was accepted, but with great reluctance. No one was happy with it
even as work on it went on, and some officials high in the Esso
organization fumed when it was presented.

Act II starts with the words of Emerson, hearing the whistle
of the locomotive in the woods, heralding the elimination of
the forests as the burgeoning industrial giant awakens. Significantly, this is one of only four moments in the program when
a writer who is not classifiable as "contemporary" (i.e., twentieth century) is used. Whitman gets quoted and is also the
subject in part of the Ginsberg poem—which sees him "poking
among the meats in the refrigerator and eyeing the grocery
boys." Mark Twain is used twice, once in his most cynical mood
and once when he comments on *homo sapiens* in general, not
on Americans in particular. Samuel Sewall is introduced in
Act III, with George C. Scott's portrayal of him hammering
again on a cynical note. So, by eliminating the sweep of commentary on America and things American that sweeps through
the eighteenth and nineteenth centuries, he who compiled the
program introduced an interesting distortion, one that elimi-

nates almost totally the three things that any competent analyst of the American experience would feel essential for inclusion—America as a unique historical experience; America as a unique civilization under unusual conditions of freedom; and the creation of that distinctive creature *The American*, the creature Hector St. Jean de Crevecoeur called the New Man. Auden gets included, validly, with his portrayal of the contented "organization man," a statistic, the "Mass Man." But he might better have been included by a recitation of a statement made to a shipboard reporter in 1948, on contemporary American literature, which would have summed up a large part of what did get included in the program:

> Coming from Europe, my first, my strongest, my most abiding impression is that no body of literature, written at any time or in any place, is so uniformly depressing. It is a source of continual astonishment to me that the nation which has the worldwide reputation of being the most optimistic, the most gregarious, and the freest on earth should see itself through the eyes of its most sensitive members as a society of helpless victims, shady characters, and displaced persons. . . .

Obviously, trumpeted chauvinism would be misplaced in a program such as this. That is precisely what we usually get in television. The Auden quotation *I* suggest would at least have underlined what the program obliquely suggests—which is that a major paradox in our culture is the tension between official optimism and the prevailing pessimism exhibited by many of our writers. When I muttered about the program's shortcomings to Gilbert Seldes a few days after its presentation, he remarked that in his own green-and-salad-days he had been instrumental in mounting a seven reel documentary on the social and economic follies of the 1920's. It was titled *This Is America*. "I meant by the title," said Seldes, "that this is what America has come to be."

Looked at this way, the title *In What America?* may be regarded as a way of underlining the pluralistic society we have, and the items exhibited may be looked upon as somehow demonstrating that essential variety.

I have no desire to be unduly harsh on a bit of experimental television programing. God knows, we get little enough of it. But it is hard for me to put down the feeling that *In What America?* failed to achieve the balance it should have achieved. The best about us is just not given enough prominence in the program.

The only President who is mentioned is Coolidge, and he is mentioned after Auden's poem has given us the Modern-Man-as-a-Statistical-Nonentity and is introduced with Mencken's words:

> Democracy is that system of government under which the people, having 35,717,342 native-born adults to choose from, including thousands who are handsome and many who are wise, pick out a Coolidge to be head of State. It is as if a hungry man, set before a banquet prepared by master cooks and covering an acre in area, should turn his back upon the feast and stay his stomach by catching and eating flies.[2]

There can be no objection to citing Coolidge, even in this light and for this purpose. But where in the program is Lincoln? Or Theodore Roosevelt? Or FDR? If Mencken on democracy is to be heard, Jefferson on the same subject is virtually mandatory. We get Thomas Wolfe's assertion that we are lost but will be found—this delivered by George C. Scott against a rear-projection of the heads of a crowd, which effectively prepares us for Auden's poem. But perhaps we should also have been given that fragment from Wolfe that appears in his last novel, part of a letter written to a character named Foxhall Edwards and setting forth an element about American pragmatism and optimism that we need:

> Man was born to live, to suffer, and to die, and what befalls him is a tragic lot. There is no denying this in the final end. But we must, dear Fox, deny it all along the way.[3]

---

[2] H. L. Mencken, "Definitions," *Prejudices: A Selection* (New York: Vintage Books, Alfred A. Knopf, 1958), p. 213.

[3] Thomas Wolfe, *You Can't Go Home Again* (New York: Harper and Row, 1940), p. 737.

We are given Harry Golden's tribute to the strength and purity of his immigrant mother, an eloquent bit and one that serves to introduce into the program fleetingly one of the greatest of American facts, that America's greatness derives from its being a somewhat special blend of many ethnic strains, that we are indeed what Whitman said we were, "a nation of nations." But perhaps we ought also to have had Edgar Lee Masters' "Lucinda Matlock." We are given Bette Davis and Rubirosa. But perhaps we ought also to have been given Helen Hayes and Robert E. Lee.

We could, obviously, not be given *any more* than we were given within fifty-three minutes, only something different. Addition is not the problem. Subtraction and replacement are. And what could well have been replaced was anything that did not focus with some precision—and totally—on the condition of America or the peculiar characteristics of Americans. Unless this was to be the principle of inclusion or exclusion in compiling the contents of the program, the title should have been shifted—to *Out of America*, for instance—in which case anything from John Dillinger's dying gasp to Nathan Hale's words at the bottom of the scaffold become eligible for entry, and a potpourri principle is established that will embrace anything and everything from Norman Mailer's soldier in *The Naked and the Dead* crying "Goddam carrion, that's all we are, men, goddam carrion" to Wallace Stevens' "Poetry is the statement of a relationship between a man and the world," a statement which would then truly permit the inclusion of American commentary on the universal conditions of men as well as the purely national ones.

I do not wish to overemphasize the distortion which the program reflects. And my dissatisfaction over its design and the lopsidedness of its content must not be interpreted to mean that I do not see in it much of value, recommend its being shown and used widely in American classrooms, and applaud some of its parts as superlative presentations of bits from American writers. We can learn as much from bad art as from good. But the distortion is there, and not to note that it is there—and to deprecate the fact—is a dangerous business. I take seriously what Santayana once said: "To be an American is of itself almost a moral condition, an education, and a career." And I regret that in putting together the hour the producers did not choose to keep more firmly in mind some classic statement of the very theme they announced, a few sentences from Gunnar Myrdal's *An American Dilemma* (Rev. ed.; New York: Harper and Row, 1962), for instance, in which, echoing the kind of approach to analyzing American society which Harriet Martineau had utilized a century earlier, Myrdal pointed out that the United States exhibits

> the ever raging conflict between, on one hand, the valuations preserved on the general plane which we shall call the "American Creed," where the American thinks, talks, and acts under the influence of high national and Christian precepts, and on the other hand, the valuations on specific planes of individual and group living, where personal and local interests; economic, social, and sexual jealousies; considerations of community prestige and conformity; group prejudices against particular persons or types of people; and all sorts of miscellaneous wants, impulses, and habits dominate his outlook.

In What America? has to stand charged with giving us almost none of the first except to poke fun at it, and a plethora of items which loosely apply to the second but do not illustrate it with anything like precision. Artistically the program fails both because it really has no focus and because, in attempting to find one, it overlooks the most salient aspects of the American character. The "America" it gives us, consequently, is a woefully incomplete one, resembling, shall we say, Old Glory complete with blue field and fifty stars but lacking the essential red stripes.

IV

John Ruskin, writing on the essentials of composition, once noted that "the most simple and perfect connection of lines is by radiation; that is, by their all springing from one point, or

closing towards it." It is a point which the producer of an hour
program for television needs to emblazon on the walls of his
workroom, lighting candles of adoration and worship to it
frequently and bowing low before it as the most essential of
his artistic credos. And certainly the producer of such programs as the *Esso World Theatre* series ignores this precept at
his peril.

Soyinka, in fashioning the script for *Nigeria: Culture in
Transition*, embraced the principle completely. He saw that
by concentrating exclusively on the interplay between the
traditional and the new, he could say something profound
about both. And in the process he could exhibit, for all to see,
the strength, the vitality, the essential health of the burgeoning
Nigerian modern culture. The problems involved in exploring
the cultural heritage of a people in an hour are formidable ones,
and he resolved his quandary principally by choosing a sufficiently tight theme so that the perils of almost inevitable superficiality, omnipresent in a venture such as this, were successfully avoided. When his hour was over, we knew where we
had been, why we had been taken there, and what we were
supposed to have seen while in his company.

Little of this can be said for *In What America?*. In fairness,
it must be said that Soyinka's task was an easier one than that
facing the anthology-maker charged with preparing the American segment of the series. Soyinka's is a new nation, if one
with an ancient heritage, but it is a heritage sufficiently circumscribed as an entity to allow efficient handling. And he
started his task with the built-in advantage of possessing
material that he knew would appeal to an American audience
because of its novelty, its exotic quality, its being illustrative
of something in which thoughtful Americans at the moment
are vitally interested, the status of the culture of the emerging
nations. But the script-preparer for *In What America?* could
have avoided much that can now be charged against him had
he embraced the same trinity that Soyinka did—the choice
of a properly tight theme; a zealous selection of material precisely illustrating that theme and arranged to illustrate it so

that, following Ruskin's dictum, it radiated and focused back at one and the same time on the one idea; and, finally, a determination that artiness, even phoniness, be shunned like the plague.

Enough, perhaps, has been said about the first two of these, but it might be pointed out additionally that a different and perhaps better way of ordering the dual material composing the program's content might have been to take a wholly negative, or wholly positive, approach in selecting the material to be presented via recitation or dramatization, then to counterbalance this with a running commentary showing the superficiality, the wrongheadedness, or the distortion from truth, if any, involved. Since American writers have been more inclined to criticize than to applaud, I would favor the negative, opening up a rich literature of national self-exploration and caustic comment produced by Americans about America from James Fenimore Cooper on, with an intelligent dialogue accompanying it as narration, one that embodied some of the yeasaying that is also a valid part of the dichotomy.

Missing too in *In What America?* is anything resembling appropriate recognition of man's essential closeness to the earth, specifically calling for some celebration of what Max Lerner once called the fact that "the tutelary divinities of land and water watched over America's destinies." This need not be a celebration of the wonders and variety of the American landscape or cerebrations over the validity or lack of validity of Turner's thesis about the frontier. But the program cries out for an inclusion of something akin to Willa Cather's opening sentence in *O Pioneers:* "One January day, thirty years ago, the little town of Hanover, anchored on a windy Nebraska tableland, was trying not to be blown away."

What *In What America?* primarily gives us is a pseudosophisticated, restricted, and decidedly metropolitan viewpoint on America, one seen from a large urban center and with the sort of contact with the actual America, both of present actuality and of heritage, that one can glean from poking amidst the piles of paperbacks in a 42nd Street bookstore, looking for tidbits that will adumbrate the thesis that we are mixed-up, drifting, or even lost souls.

What *In What America?* cries for, in short, is the sort of unifying and tightly controlled theme that Martin Duberman utilized in putting into shape for dramatization the procession of historical documents that are given to us in his *In White America*, which seems to me to be the best—thus far—of the attempts to hack out something of a new theatrical genre, what Duberman calls a "documentary play" or "a play out of historical documents." In doing so, Duberman recognizes that, as he puts it, "professional history, which aims at the comprehensive, and professional theatre, which relies on the selective, are at cross-purposes." Yet, he also recognizes (and achieves his goal in surmounting it) that the two can be cross-bred to produce both good history and satisfactory theater, even superlative theater since the theater is almost never better than when it is mirroring fact but doing so in a highly dramatic context. It is a format that lends itself to television even better than to the theater, and we can only hope that we are given more experiments akin to those I have been exploring here that are close to it. Television desperately needs its own forms, it being a medium that took over the time blocs of radio and that has borrowed or mirrored so far almost exclusively the forms perfected for the movies, for the stage, for the variety theater, for the documentary on film. This new genre might be television's own. But in perfecting it, television will have to learn carefully the lessons implicit in the structure of the two programs I have dealt with.

And, perhaps most important of all, it must—to go back to the trinity dealt with above—eschew phony artiness in putting together the format for such ventures. *In What America?* reeks of it, from its excessively fragmented presentation sans connective links, through its supposedly "American" dances created by Katherine Durham (but no more evocative of the essential America than the Watusi would be), to its jazz background.

Artiness, in short, destroyed, at least for me, much of the

effectiveness of the program. George C. Scott, interviewed by
a New York *Times* reviewer about the show, pointed out,
"No, we don't sit on stools and read. No such pretentious sim-
plicity." But what about the effectiveness of *elaborate pre-
tentiousness*—Emerson's words heard against the background
of a dancer poised on the top of a ladder, doing a kind of ballet-
of-stretched-nether-limbs; or Faulkner's Nobel Prize acceptance speech, delivered by George C. Scott in the manner of
Thornton Wilder's stage manager in *Our Town*? There was
none of this in Soyinka's show, except momentarily when the
Off-Broadway couple read the modern Nigerian poetry *perched
on stools*, and it was handled well. The producer of *In What
America?* would have been well advised to free his cameras
from the studio, providing footage of the actual America to
reach our eyes as we listened to his readers. Or, being really
daring, to assume that the kind of Americans who will watch
this type of show are capable of listening alone and are not in
need of a three-ring circus to hold their attention.

I watched the program for the third time alone in a projection booth with a television producer who detests the arty as
much as I do, and at its conclusion he turned to me and said:
"The director is too visible in this thing. All of his preferences
are on display." He was right. Really good art hides such
matters.

V

One cannot dissect a set of offerings such as these without
running the risk, and it is a considerable one, of courting te-
dium. The criticism of television especially runs this risk
because television is so evanescent. The critic can rarely assume that more than a fraction of his readers have *seen* the
program he chooses to impale on his cutting board. Or much
of what television presents is so trivial that criticizing it seems
worthless—"How could I," said a Chicago critic, "stay sane if
I tried to review *Bonanza* weekly!"

In preparing the several sections of this volume, its authors were asked specifically to relate the areas of their concern to the uses which teachers of English might make of them. As a teacher of English, but one who regards the world of film and television as now also part of his concern, I take this charge with special seriousness. How, then, can *Culture in Transition* and *In What America?* be of use, or programs like them?

At one point in my young manhood I was wont to spend an occasional hour with Ezra Pound in that period when he was incarcerated at Saint Elizabeth's Hospital in Washington, D. C., the unwilling guest of the U.S. Government. One day as we sat on the lawn, I asked him what I, as a young instructor of English, should try to convey to my students about writing and literature. "Precision, precision, precision," Pound fairly shrieked at me.

It is sound advice, for the writer as well as for the compiler of television programs. And Pound offers equally good advice in a little essay which he sent me a few days after his outburst, entitled "The Teacher's Mission," printed in his *Polite Essays* (New York: New Directions, 1937), advice that takes on new meaning in an era when the electronic medium makes such ventures as *Culture in Transition* and *Inside What America?* available for classroom analysis. "All teaching of literature," Pound writes there, "should be performed by the presentation and juxtaposition of specimens of writing and NOT by discussion of some other discusser's opinion *about* the general standing of a poet or author." He goes on to call it the "ideogramic method," and it resembles nothing so much as the method such television programs must utilize as their format. These shows are "ideogramic," then, in that they butt segment against segment, style against style, idea against idea in rapid succession, the whole supposedly structured to one overriding purpose.

The two programs I have devoted my attention to here are representative of an emerging genre, one that lends itself with particular effectiveness to the teacher's purpose, both as Pound saw it and as common sense dictates it.

It might be interesting, for instance, to put students to work manufacturing scripts for a program comparable to *In What*

America?. They should be allowed freedom to plunder our literary heritage as they wish, placing the tags and bits and pieces they collect from their voyages among the bookshelves as they wish—but then subject to the kind of close, critical scrutiny about purpose and design that is the proper critical stance. "Precision, precision, precision," as Pound would shout.

David Boroff

Television and the Problem Play

One of the more tenacious notions about our culture is that theater is "serious," while television—the land of the fadeproof smile—offers mere entertainment. This beguiling idea has enabled many theater-goers, for whom the evening in midtown is simply a middle class ritual, to maintain feelings of lofty superiority over the great mass of television viewers, who, beer can in hand, journey through vast subcontinents of junk.

The trouble with this pat formulation is that it does not agree with the realities. First, there is no such thing as *mere* entertainment. Even in the zaniest episode of a situation comedy, there are thematic implications. If television is often innocent of ideas, it is never devoid of attitudes and values. *Beverly Hillbillies,* for example, is nothing more than a calculatedly silly situation comedy. Yet it offers the standard myths of populist reassurance: the superior wisdom of the unlettered; the fecklessness of the upper class; the gaiety of the ignorant; the pompous solemnity of the rich. Since television is ubiquitous and immeasurably powerful, educators ought to pay attention even to the most trivial shows, for even triviality does not exclude attitudes and points of view.

But there is another level of television programing—the serious drama—which invites comparison with the theater. In fact, it is safe to say that the roles of TV and theater have been curiously reversed. Today it is television that is the more serious medium, while theater—except for a handful of honorable exceptions each season—has become mere expense account divertissement or somewhat irrelevant avant-garde doodling. Theater has largely abandoned that large middle area of common experience which was its metier. The "smash," every producer's daydream, is almost always a musical rather than a serious drama. And production costs are so high that producers must do what Hollywood has been doing for a long time—run as few risks as possible in order not to alienate their comfortable middle class audience in quest of an evening's titillation.

TV, on the other hand, has become almost doggedly homiletic. While theater these days settles for entertainment, television has been, almost since its inception, a vast electronic classroom. There is a tendency to lament the passing of venturesome live drama—*Playhouse 90*, *Kraft*, etc.—but though television may be more formula-ridden than before, it is no less didactic. And the burden of teaching Americans how to live was asumed by the regular series such as *The Defenders*, *Nurses and Doctors*, *Ben Casey*, etc., which week after week relentlessly tackled the domestic problems that beset Americans.

How has this role come about? It is partly the peculiar sociology of television, partly a legacy from earlier literary forms. Viewed sociologically, television represents the most pervasive of mass media on which a heavy burden of social responsibility has been imposed. Unlike the movies, there has been public and official scrutiny of TV from the beginning. Moreover, it is a rich sector of our economy with marked overtones of respectability and piety. (Hollywood and even radio by contrast were raffish in their early days.) Even if total frivolity were possible, the so-called creative people in the medium would not settle for it. Among them are many cultivated people—intellectuals, failed intellectuals, ex-intellectuals along with the fringe people that a new medium inevitably attracts. Such people zealously pursue meaning. Many of them, mindful of the power and affluence of TV, feel guilty about the medium's abuses and genuinely want to make a social contribution. TV's didacticism better enables its practitioners to endure their prosperity. And it is too easy a temptation to dismiss this as sanctimoniousness or opportunism, easier still to reject their efforts as aesthetically inept.

But what we shall have to call "the problem play" derives from a long and honorable literary tradition—that of middle class domestic drama, which reached its apogee in the late nineteenth and early twentieth centuries. Ernest Kinoy, Robert Alan Aurthur, and Alvin Boretz are the legitimate heirs of Henrik Ibsen, Sidney Howard, and Arthur Miller. (As the more sophisticated medium abandons an enterprise, the popular medium adopts it.) But it might be equally to the point to trace television drama to a somewhat older ancestor: the sentimental novel of the late eighteenth and nineteenth centuries, which also set out to instruct a new middle class in the management of their lives. From Samuel Richardson through Charles Dickens, there is a strong cautionary and hortatory bent. Richardson instructs young ladies in how to protect their virtue and the heavy cost of capitulating to vice. Dickens, a real precursor of television in his vast popularity, is the great persuader who rouses the comfortable and the uncaring to new social sympathies in much the same fashion as television would mobilize sentiment later on for minority groups, the physically and emotionally handicapped, the forlorn and the distressed, the poor and the disadvantaged.

One need only cite some of the long-term programs on TV to suggest the range and depth of their social concerns. Within its own drastic limits, television is a civilizing agency, at least an acculturating one. *East Side/West Side* showed a sympathy for the economically deprived long before President Johnson enunciated his poverty program. (It also provided orientation in how social agencies operate.) *Eleventh Hour* offered basic training in the uses of psychiatry: what to do until the doctor arrives. *The Defenders* gave pointers in the law and often maturely explored the conflicts between human rights and legal rights. *Ben Casey* and *Dr. Kildare* provided insights into the dilemmas of everyday medical practice. But all of these "problem" series converge in their basic and oft-repeated ideology. They argue on behalf of a generalized middle class ethic which will enable us to get through the tense, troubled, and crowded sixties. It is by no means a noble ethic or even a very demanding one. What television says—and says again and again—is: Be tolerant; try to understand the other fellow; accept your own limitations and the limitations of other people. It doesn't countenance extravagant or self-indulgent action. What society requires, TV seems to say, is not visionaries or heroes or saints but sensible, moderate people, their neuroses firmly under control. In other words, television teaches us not so much how to live but how to put up with the lives we have to live.

Nothing underlines this quite so vividly, perhaps, as the role of the elder in TV drama. Typically, in the series, there is a headstrong young man whose passion for justice—construed in simple, stark terms—is held in check, or tempered, by the cautious wisdom of an older guide. The older man has learned the sad truth of complexity, the sluggish pace of progress, the inevitability of defeat. Thus Ben Casey has his Zorba, Kildare is checkmated by Gillespie, Mr. Novak is shadowed by a principal, as Ken Preston is by his father—judicious guides, all of them, through the thickets of experience.

Because television is so preeminently a spokesman for a kind of sensible accommodation to society, it is often betrayed into curious contradictions. In the traditional problem play, the individual is pitted against society, and though he is often defeated, there is no doubt about where justice lies. TV, however, is constantly reconciling the claims of conflicting groups, and the television drama typically ends in a cautious hedge, a muted compromise, a victory so qualified it often looks like defeat. Similarly, defeat on TV is often qualified out of existence. Life's dilemmas succumb to the *deus ex machina*.

It is not difficult to provide examples of the shrinking from hard answers that is often characteristic of television. A few years ago, there was an episode on *Nurses and Doctors* which considered the case of a call girl hospitalized for a heart attack. Drama develops when the young woman, previously regarded

as a model, acknowledges that she is a prostitute. Bedside solicitude vanishes at once. The student nurses, bundles of whole-
someness until now, are full of prurient curiosity. A young
resident who had obviously been smitten by the young "model"
is now grimly moralistic. But liberal good will—TV's staple
commodity—takes over. The student nurses settle back into
straight-faced professionalism. The head nurse—a Wise Elder—
castigates the resident for his priggishness. Full of remorse,
the resident rushes off to apologize to the call girl who has
already checked out of the hospital. And now we come to TV's
dilemma: Does the call girl elicit the same mental hygiene
dispensation as the juvenile delinquent, the junkie, the men-
tally sick, the divorced, and the suicidal? Or is she too threatening to middle class stability for that? Can vice be rewarded
with kindness? Has TV gone hipster on us? In the end, the
script utilizes the oldest dodge in *kitsch*. The young physician
intercepts the call girl as she is leaving her handsomely fur-
nished East Side bagnio. (She has just been discharged as a
bad health risk: What if she should have another heart attack
while in the company of an important client?) As the young
resident mumbles his Hippocratic apologies, she is stricken
with another heart attack and dies in his arms. Before she
does, each has learned something: she, that the world is not
really a jungle; he, that it is. In any event, the day is saved for
tolerance, but nobody has to face up to life with Clarissa.

Another example of equivocation was provided by *Channing*,
a series about a college campus. *Channing*, in its very conception, demonstrated both what is right and what is wrong about
TV; it was a vivid enactment of the way contradictory impulses
—the desire to make a useful social comment and the urge to
play safe—cancel each other out. In its original concept, *Channing* was to dramatize the new role of the university as a locus
of power, the crossroads where ideas, technical expertise, politics, and the arts converged. (The pilot program was a reason-
ably faithful adaptation of Lionel Trilling's superb short story,
"Of This Time, Of That Place.") Unhappily, its rationale under-
went a striking transformation—its good intentions were un-

dercut, its sophistication badly watered down, and its sense of milieu grievously distorted.

Television is, indeed, a teacher of reality, but the reality it teaches is often out of date. Fearful of outstripping its constituency, TV often settles for stale stereotypes, outworn images, received notions. What it comes down to is that TV has an infuriating habit of summoning up its courage, taking a deep breath, and then emitting a puny little squeak. Thus, in *Channing*, the controlling image of the university as the new powerhouse of our society was scrapped in favor of the traditional elm-shaded campus where other worldly types pursue Platonic essences and engage in earnest colloquy with colleagues and students. There is hardly a hint in it of the new purse-proud academia with its fat grants, its junkets, its experts in demand everywhere—and, yes, its indifference, if not downright contempt for undergraduate teaching. The protagonist, too, is correspondingly anachronistic. Joseph Howe is the very stereotype of the high-minded but feckless professor —bookish, gentle, and ineffective. We have been spared only the pipe and the tweeds. There is little suggestion that professors know their way around these days. The vintage is that of 1936 not 1963.

An episode on *Channing*, "Message from a Tin Room," dealt with a young thug who was convicted of murder and is awaiting execution. During his incarceration, he wrote a powerful testament which has come to Howe's attention. Having been caught up in the manuscript, Howe visits the condemned man in prison and feels implicated in the convict's destiny. The thug is all fire and passion, a fallen proletarian angel, whose intensities only underscore the professor's pallor. "When I saw a guy with a briefcase," the convict cries out, "I wanted to kill him. The buildings mocked me. The briefcases shamed me." Determined to save the condemned man, Howe drives to the state capitol to plead with the governor. But he fails, and the convict has to die in the "tin room." But the anguish is greater, not less, because of what has recently passed between the two men. The convict has a new fulfillment—as a writer—but it is too late.

"I gave him something to live for," Howe says. "To die with nothing to live for is cruel. Think how much worse it is to die with everything to live for."

The real issue in this episode of *Channing* is capital punishment, and the real life event in its background is the Caryl Chessman case. But here television executes one of its nimble retreats. As the hour of the convict's execution approaches, Howe is inconsolable. But his dean comes along with bromidic optimism, arguing that "there could be no other chronology." Had there been no incarceration and impending execution, there would have been no manuscript. Pangloss himself could not have phrased it better. "We have to stop manufacturing murderers," the dean concludes piously and somewhat irrelevantly. Duly reconciled to things as they are, Howe trots off to his staff room and to the next set of freshman themes.

A similar blurring of reality—under the guise of a new suburbanized social realism—was the case, too, with *Mr. Novak*. Here again, the intentions were wholesome, the execution less than admirable. One quickly perceived that the intent of Mr. Novak was to upend all the unsavory stereotypes of the male teacher which we have inherited from the past. If the male teacher was vaguely epicene, he was now redoubtably masculine, heartbreakingly good-looking. If in the past, his morale as a male schoolmarm was weak—if, indeed, he suffered from self-contempt—he was now buoyant and committed and upbeat, the very portrait of the new teacher-executive. If in the old view, male teachers daydreamed about getting into something more lucrative, in *Mr. Novak* they would rather fight than switch.

There was so much nobility in Jefferson High—the locale of *Mr. Novak*—it makes one cringe. Mr. Novak himself had the grim earnestness—and also the naive moralism—of a West Point cadet. The principal was yet another of the Wise Elders who swarm all over the networks, full of solicitude and sententiousness ("I think as you grow older you will discover that everyone has a little insecurity in him"). And the teachers were unswervingly conscientious, devoting their free periods to im-

promptu seminars on pedagogy. Notably absent (except perhaps as a "problem") was that healthy, abrasive cynicism that
enables teachers to hang on to their sanity.

An episode early in 1964 exhibited both Mr. Novak's good
will and neutralizing timidity in the face of conventional values.
The drama concerns a passionately bookish but unhappy boy
who in the conformist climate of Jefferson High is regarded
as something of a freak. Stung by his lack of popularity, he
commits some minor delinquencies. Breaking into the school's
trophy room, he smashes some holy ikons—basketball and
track awards he could never hope to win. He also moons calf-
ishly under the window of a cute little thing to whom he is too
shy to say "hi." He otherwise occupies himself with browsing
in a local bookstore. It is in this book-lined sanctuary that Mr.
Novak looks for the boy when the latter seems to be in trouble.
Ultimately, Mr. Novak takes the boy under his wing and reads
his outsized manuscript. (The boy is the sort who lies in wait
for his teachers in gloomy stairwells as he clutches a fat manuscript oozing adolescent *weltschmerz*.) The therapy works,
and we see the boy returning to the bosom of the adolescent
community, even managing a cheery "hi" to the little nymphet
whom earlier he was at the point of molesting.

Under the guise of promoting good will and understanding,
this episode actually does some mischief. For one thing, bookishness is hardly a problem today when National Merit Schol-
ars are the real heroes of high school, not the athletes. (If there
is a problem, it is that of the nonacademic boy for whom there
is no way out these days.) Moreover, if the bookish boy is
unhappy, the answer is not necessarily to find a safe haven in
the adolescent subculture. His need is not to find his way *back*
but to find his way. Mr. Novak is obviously sympathetic to
bookishness but not at the expense of adjustment. He seems to
overlook that there may well be more important things than
saying "hi" to a pretty classmate.

Programs such as those I have just discussed—however vulnerable to criticism—present a real opportunity for the classroom teacher. What is often overlooked is that a bad program

can be almost as valuable as a good one in helping students define criteria. Television has been charged with narcotizing the American public. It is true that one can be stunned into insensibility by endless din, by Byzantine variations of the same plots, and even by repetitive preachments. But the autonomous viewer can be lulled and gulled only insofar as he chooses to be. If TV is to fulfill its potentialities, it must have an alert, vigilant, ruthlessly critical audience. And the natural place for the training of that audience is in the high school (even in the elementary school), where intellectual snobbery has not yet been consolidated. Instead of its blunting the student's sense of reality, television can reinvigorate it—if the classroom teacher poses the right questions. In effect, students have to become cultural critics attuned to such questions as the following: What is the relationship between what the program describes and the actuality? What does the drama *say* about American life? What attitudes are implicit in it? How does it illuminate the American life-style or the American character? How effective is the program artistically?

Fortunately, not all TV dramas represent evasions or distortions of reality or tricky footwork in dodging issues. There are some problem-oriented series that are honorably exempt from the strictures and reservations expressed above. These programs often project a maturity of vision, a moral probity, and an intellectual toughness that justify the medium and vindicate the claim made earlier that TV has largely taken over the function, previously exercised by theater, of exploring social reality. Students can discover how to identify them.

There are, of course, taboos and limitations. Unlike theater, television cannot explore new frontiers of experience. Themes like homosexuality and drug addiction are approached from a rigidly conventional point of view. It is hard to imagine a play like *The Connection* being done on TV; it even took courage to telecast *The Iceman Cometh*, which exploits exploits sex and degradation but hardly flouts conventional values. And because television is geared to a mass audience, there are sharp limitations in intellectual density and in richness and complexity of ideas and language. Moreover, the economics of the industry is such that script writers have a relatively short time in which to hammer out a script. Often TV plays sound better than they are because of skillful acting and expert direction, but one need only read a script critically to see that its strength rarely lies in texture or beauty of language.

During the last few years, the best of the series were *Naked City*, *East Side/West Side*, and *The Defenders*. (It is a melancholy comment on the medium that these programs have fallen victim to the infamous rating system.) In its heyday, *Naked City* was distinguished by an exquisite urban sensitivity. Crime stories are, in essence, post-problem plays because the criminal act itself demonstrates the breakdown of the dialectic of the problem. When a crime is committed, there can no longer be discussion, only detection and punishment. But in its attitudes towards its characters—both law-breakers and enforcers—*Naked City* had links to the great tradition of Western literature. There was as much Dostoyevski as there was Dashiel Hammett in *Naked City*, far more Chekhov than Hemingway. The episodes in *Naked City* were not always clearly identified as problem plays, but certainly the characters were problematical.

Nothing could be more instructive than a contrast between *The Untouchables*, which purveyed precisely the kind of mindless violence that appalls the critics of TV, and *Naked City*, which offered not so much violence as psychic disorders. Where *The Untouchables* was almost pornographically violent, the violence in *Naked City* was a sometime thing—harshly eruptive, nervous, graceless, unhappy. And the malefactors were not romantic rebels but perambulating case histories, their psychic lesions plain to see. With them crime was not a willed act of insurgency but rather a surge of desperation, an inchoate protest against a society whose ways are at once mysterious and ruinous. And the crime itself—shabby, misguided, often pointless—was enacted against the most squalid background this side of a documentary. It always seemed to be winter in *Naked City*—remorselessly gray days, the very buildings oozing a clammy cold while bulky middle-aged men shuffled in heavy overcoats.

The police in *Naked City* also provided a striking contrast to the lawmen in *The Untouchables*. Eliot Ness and his cohorts were men of stone, absolutely implacable. In fact, they played the gangsters' own game of graceful, stylized violence from the other side of the fence. The police in *Naked City*, however, were gentle creatures—almost disabled by pity—with an infinite capacity for being pained. As much social workers as cops, they bore witness to man's folly and anguish.

It was the close of *Naked City* that always defined its tone. For at that moment, police and law-breaker shared a common martyrdom: the criminal for what he had done, the police who bundled the culprit into the squad car, social workers who had failed. What did *Naked City* say? One of its strengths was that it said nothing which is neatly paraphrasable. It was, in truth, Chekhovian in its rueful gaze at people in the clutch of disaster. *Naked City* was, in essence, a compassionate—not a savage—eye. This I have seen, it said.

Among some "insiders" in television, *East Side/West Side* was viewed as a successor to *Naked City*. A series about a social worker, *East Side/West Side* reflected a kind of urban melancholy and was disinclined to pretty up the untidy facts of existence. There were the same peeling tenement flats as in *Naked City*, the bedraggled people sitting on the stoops, the choking passions of the inarticulate. Moreover, though Brock, the social worker, was by profession a meliorist, there was more often than not a sense of irresolution when his efforts came to a close. (In this respect, *East Side/West Side* contrasted with some of the medical and psychiatric series in which the curtain is almost always rung down on a firm, invincible answer.) Brock tried, God knows, but he was almost paralyzed by the odds against him and by an almost Gogolian sense of the inertia, bureaucratic sloth, and indifference arrayed against him.

George C. Scott as Brock was admirably cast. No prim do-gooder, he had the worn, battered look of a man who has not only seen it all but done it all. Unmarried, himself living on the fringe, he had the aura of a secular priest, consecrated by his work but forever mindful of the frailty of man. Hard-bitten, unillusioned, he squinted in helpless misery at all the misery out there.

One of the very best of the episodes on *East Side/West Side* was on display early in 1964. "No Hiding Place" dealt with Negroes moving into a formerly all white suburb, and it confronted the problem without any of the polite evasions that have characterized excursions of the mass media into this troubled area. In fact, it nailed one of the lies that are athwart in any real communication between the races: the implicit insistence by white people, as a condition for integration, upon the White Negro—the Negro who conforms to the white man's genteel expectations.

"No Hiding Place" deals with an attractive white couple in the suburbs. He is gregarious, a little sloppy with money, superficially liberal. She is a sweet young thing from the South whose conscience nags at her inherited racism. Their neighbors are garden variety suburbanites with the usual predilection for barbecue pits and PTA meetings. A Negro family moves in— an eminently suitable one with M.I.T. in the background, meticulous speech, and well-mannered children. Panic ensues anyway. The crabgrass vigilantes are certain that property values will collapse, and blockbusters, portrayed with undisguised malice, move in to capitalize on their fears. But Brock turns up too and tries to keep the suburbanites' nerves under control by making them understand that it is up to them—if they don't bolt, property values will hold up, and all will be well.

At this point, a tidy, comforting resolution would have been entirely in order. Even die-hard exclusionists will accept one well-qualified Negro family. But the script takes the hard way out. To dispose of the house of a white defector, the Negro couple recommends a friend. He proves to be a self-made man, likeable enough but crude and uneducated, who innocently violates most of the genteel norms of the community. The nightmare fears come flooding back. For Brock, the focal point of this resurgent hysteria is the young couple. "All right, you wanted a white Negro," he tells them, "and you got a black one." And that is precisely the way the issue has to be defined. At the play's end, the lines are being stringently drawn in the community with Brock on hand to prop up the faltering and victory by no means assured. Meanwhile, the young couple have undergone an Ibsenic sea-change. The little ninny, no longer living in her Dixie doll house, has discovered unexpected resources within herself, while her blowhard husband, all liberal platitude before, has edged towards racist hostility when the chips are down.

"No Hiding Place" is right-minded without being sanctimonious, crisp and economical without oversimplifying. And it has touches of mordant humor which soften the social preachment. Ruby Dee as the young wife in the "acceptable" Negro family is asked by a well-meaning dolt whether she prefers Louis Armstrong or Miles Davis. "I dig Bach and Mozart," she replies acidly.

The problem series which combined both durability and a sturdy social conscience is *The Defenders*, perhaps the best series on the air for a time. (It is no small achievement for a program with any serious intentions to survive on TV. Witness the notoriously low ratings of culturally ambitious and public interest programs.) In its few years of existence, *The Defenders* explored a wide range of human justice and the majesty of the law; the program ranged itself on the side of the law. And this was dramatized through the struggle, in familiar TV fashion, between Wise Elder and Young Turk. The older Preston, Lawrence, was Solomonic in his sobriety and good sense; his son, Ken, was full of reformist zeal which his father must constantly curb. Unlike *East Side/West Side*, where the social workers seemed immersed in the woes of the world, the attorneys in *The Defenders* were depicted as rather proper, privileged Ivy League types who found themselves occasionally lapped by waves of misery. But there could be no doubt about either their decency or their genuine, if somewhat remote, human sympathies. Even when the older Preston insisted upon the primacy of law, it was never done smugly, and almost always with a sense of how the law can miscarry.

One of the prime virtues of *The Defenders* was that it did not shrink from controversial issues. The Prestons brought to bear on these issues a kind of upper class coolness, a commitment to traditional liberties, and a talent for seeing the other man's point of view. Sometimes this could lead to a kind of barbarous rationalism as in the episode about an ex-Nazi death camp physician who in this country has become an outstanding medical practitioner. When he is murdered by one of his victims, the program takes pains to make an elaborate case for the ex-Nazi: he did the job he had to do, he made both life and death easier for the concentration camp inmates, in this country he was an exemplary citizen, etc. But on other issues, the program is staunch and unambiguous in its commitments. Thus, in a recent episode about an agnostic who teaches in a private school, the Prestons enable the man to keep his job and his dignity when both are threatened. One could almost use *The Defenders* as a barometer of suburban opinion. One could safely infer that among solid, college-educated people, agnosticism is no longer viewed as a social disease.

Perhaps the most skillful and vigorously argumentative of episodes on *The Defenders* concerned the blacklist in the entertainment industry. To be sure, the episode made its appearance in 1964 when blacklisting fever had declined. One would be more impressed by TV if the industry itself had not participated in blacklisting and if it had offered this critique of the practice a decade ago when blacklisting had epidemic proportions. Still one must be grateful for courage and social decencies whenever one finds them.

"Blacklist," written by Ernest Kinoy, is superb television drama. It deals forthrightly and maturely with complicated issues, it reflects a shrewd sense of character, and it projects a humane point of view which is never labored. To be sure, it is not really literature. There is something about the elliptical, swift-paced style of television writing—the necessity to encompass a great deal in fifty minutes—which is inimical to the creation of genuine literature. The building blocks of literature are words, and imaginative, richly textured language is the most expendable thing of all on TV. One may safely say that television plays will, in future years, be of far more interest to the cultural historian or anthropologist than to the literary scholar.

The principal virtue of "Blacklist" is that it touches all bases. It succeeds in encompassing many points of view although its own position is clear. We see the problem not only from the vantage point of the blacklisted actor but from that of his family, the beleaguered producer, the small-town politician, and even the professional patrioteer who sets the blacklisting in motion. What is more, there are no moral monsters in the unfolding of the play. But what does emerge is an inexorable process—blacklisting—which once initiated develops a kind of sinister autonomy.

The climate of "Blacklist" is the thaw, our own time when movie producers have begun to think that the blacklisting madness is over. In the office of an obscure independent producer, the name Joe Larch comes up as possible casting for a small part in a projected movie. The producer, George Veigh, decides to use him. Larch is resurrected in a shoe store where he has been working for some time. Then we see him at home—in a modest but tasteful apartment—expressing the hope that the long embargo is over. "Thank God," his wife says. And Larch whispers tenderly to her: "Thank you for everything, especially the last ten years."

But in the small town where the film is scheduled to be shot, the mimeograph machines are busy. A self-appointed vigilante group, the Vanguard League, has learned of the proposed hiring of Larch and has alerted the local citizenry ("an actor with a record of seven separate citations of Communist front affiliations"). We observe the mimeographed sheets flying out of the machine like bullets. At home, Joe Larch and his family see heaven betrayed. "Ten years . . . what do they want from you?" his wife asks. And his son, an angry activist, erupts: "You just going to let some bunch of crackpots run you out of town? I didn't understand it then, and I still don't. Why didn't you do something? Why didn't you fight back?"

In what is a classic expression of helplessness, Joe Larch explains to his son what went on in the darkest days of blacklisting:

> There was nothing to fight . . . all of a sudden nobody called . . . Nobody would tell you . . . but you just didn't get work . . . If you made trouble then . . . if you sued somebody . . . if you got yourself called in front of a committee you were dead. Even if you could win, you were "controversial." That was like leprosy. You walked down a street ringing a bell so people could get out of your way . . . Unclean . . . Unclean.

But the boy is not so easily persuaded. He wants to know: "You going to let it happen all over again? You just going to lie down?" Stung by this challenge, Larch consults Lawrence Preston to see if there is any legal recourse. And here we come to one of the cruxes of the episode: the Prestons, in their rationalistic purity, are easily misled. Men of good will, they find it difficult to conceive of people being anything else. Since Larch was never a Communist (he had participated in "liberal" causes alleged later to be Communist fronts), Lawrence Preston argues that "things can be settled sensibly" by talking to the people involved. In the meantime, the mayor of the small city where the movie is to be "shot" is beginning to panic because of the protests about Larch.

The older Preston visits Judson Kyle, the chief architect of the Vanguard League. The portrait of Kyle verges on caricature. He is given to perfervid reminiscences about 1952—"a very good year . . . we cleaned a lot of them out"—while Preston listens in stony silence. When the lawyer suggests that our laws effectively protect us against espionage and subversion, Kyle launches a paranoic tirade against "the enemy," who is everywhere. "There are only two sides," Kyle argues. "You're either for them or against them." Convinced that further discussion with Kyle would be unavailing, Preston leaves only to be intercepted by Kyle's secretary who is engaged in a discreet shakedown racket. She proposes that Larch could be "cleared" by engaging her brother, a public relations consultant.

In what was a weekly ritual on *The Defenders*, the Prestons have their own private confrontation. The son is indignant that his father would even contemplate paying off Kyle's secretary. The father takes a more tempered view. He sees Kyle as "obsessive but completely sincere." And Kyle's secretary, he argues, "didn't invent Spain or Communist Front organizations, or the Cold War." Ken is all for making a frontal attack on blacklisting itself: "If he were a narcotics addict or something, he'd be innocent until proven guilty . . . but not with the Blacklist. Nobody has to prove anything . . . all they have to do is accuse, that's enough!"

At a meeting of the small town city council, the motion to approve the movie project is tabled. This is a demonstration of what Kyle's secretary describes as the first rule of politics: "get the heat off yourself." The matter is now squarely in the lap of the producer who is terrified that he will not get financing if he retains Joe Larch. Accordingly, he has his secretary call the actor and tell him that there have been script changes and that his services will not be required. The lines are now clearly drawn.

But Lawrence Preston still believes that a solution can be achieved—"you should be able to work things out with reasonable, honest men." His son, on the other hand, still wants to press home an attack on blacklisting itself. The older Preston and Larch finally confront the producer who first tries to weasel his way out by talking nervously about "shuffling the character . . . teenage identification," irrelevancies of that sort. Then he breaks down and reveals that though nobody told him to fire Larch, there could be no approval from Mill City with Larch in the cast and therefore no movie. The producer tries to maintain a pious posture ("I suffered . . . I'm telling you, I suffered"), but Larch will give him no easy absolution: "Sure, you have it both ways now, George. You have your picture . . . and the nice comfortable feeling that you're a fine liberal man of good will."

In the end, Ken Preston does find a legal track. Larch has been deprived of his property rights as the result of an "intermeddlar"—in this case not only Judson Kyle but also the mayor and financing company all of whom put pressure on the producer not to hire Larch. It's ingenious law, the older Preston acknowledges, but it won't work because they can't prove that Judson Kyle's action was directly responsible for what happened. "Blacklisting," he points out, "goes on in a vague, poisonous fog . . . nobody tells anybody anything, they don't have to. They 'know' . . . they get the message, and you can't prove anything." Bitter and indignant, Ken decides that the law *is* an ass, as Larch's son had earlier suggested, but the older Preston attempts to palliate his son's anger:

> The Law is man-made and it's imperfect. There isn't a neat, satisfying ending to every story in life. And that goes for the Law. Sometimes everything just ends up in the air. No climax. No rescue. Not even a good rousing disaster. Just a kind of nagging trailing off into life.

"Blacklist" is polemic drama at its best. Ernest Kinoy showed both good judgment and courage in having as his blacklister (the producer) not a sinister antilibertarian but a man of flabby good will who capitulates to pressure. In any case, the insidious pattern is clearly anatomized: presure groups who shrewdly skirt the edge of libel and cause untold mischief; people of good will who knuckle under; victims deprived of a livelihood because of political and social commitments made in all innocence years earlier. The script writer displayed courage, too, in not finding a tidy resolution even if in real life, as in the celebrated case of John Henry Faulk, some performers have actually won redress.

One might quarrel with the insistently rational tone of "Blacklist." There is a Kafkaesque dimension—the fog-like quality that the older Preston refers to—in blacklisting that the play hardly exploits. In other words, instead of its being merely a statement about a social problem, "Blacklist" had the opportunity to make a larger statement about contemporary life. One quarrels, too, with the reconciliation that the older Preston provides at the end. Though it is in substance unobjectionable, it deflects the dramatic drive of the play, blunts the edge of indignation, and offers a rationale for what is clearly reprehensible.

But these are minor reservations. "Blacklist" is television at the very edge of social maturity.

Raymond Williams

Some Versions of Shakespeare on the Screen

Romeos and Juliets (Westinghouse)

You haven't got the wrong reel. The young man singing *Maria* in the introductory sequence is an allegorical Romeo, even if the name isn't quite the same. At the very beginning, we are at the point of nervousness in the television producer's presentation of Shakespeare. He is going to show us four treatments of the *Romeo and Juliet* balcony scene. Already he has extracted the most popular romantic scene from the most popular romantic play, but he's still worried. Is the decision to watch a TV program made in the first few minutes? If so, something familiar and holding, quickly. So Maria, Maria, Maria.

And then the compere explains we are to see four treatments: a scene from Gounod's opera, a modern ballet with music by Tschaikowski, a scene from *West Side Story* (for which we've already had the trailer), and, of course, Shakespeare himself. It's a good idea, and a very useful basis for thinking about convention and genre. Almost at once, however, there is a difficulty. Shakespeare himself? By this is presumably meant the words of the play, or, more precisely, the words of Act Two, Scene Two, minus the last four lines. These of course exist in print, carefully edited. But the problem of performing them is the whole problem, in an enterprise of this kind. "Shakespeare himself" begs the question, at the very beginning. What, in fact, do we actually see?

Not of course an Elizabethan stage, but the familiar unde-

fined open space of the television studio. At the center of this
space, a low balcony, with curtains behind it. The balcony is
too low for the first story of any house, and of course much
lower than the gallery of an Elizabethan stage. The dramatic
spacing is thus immediately altered: the lovers are close to
each other and, indeed, come to kiss through the balustrade. It
is a perfectly possible way of *replaying* the scene, but it is best
to get clear at the beginning that this is not Shakespeare himself. In the play, the physically dramatized closeness and separation are bridged only by words.

But this, it quickly appears, is the least of our problems.
When the actor playing Romeo begins to speak, it is difficult
to believe one's ears. Perhaps there has been some careful preliminary discussion of character, so that Romeo is "seen" and
then physically created, apart from the words, as a merry lad.
What comes through, that is to say, is a slight drunk. There is
some costume resemblance to a traditional Romeo—tradition
there meaning mainly the nineteenth century stage—but all the
gestures of face and hands and body underline a kind of adolescent tipsiness rather than even the most conventional adolescent romance. The speaking of the words underlines this impression. All the form and rhythm of the verse has disappeared
into a long running measure. One lacks a convention to render
in print the resultant medley. The unrhymed lines merely dis-
solve, while the pointed rhymed couplets produce an embar-
rassed but still unrhythmical check. Where the verse will not
run into the ordinary tipsy medley, it is cut into little hard
blocks: *Love goes toward love. As schoolboys. From their
books. But love from love. Toward school. With heavy looks.*

The rather hard Juliet is less breathless, but so sure of herself, on that little low balcony, that when she comes to say

> Thou knowest the mask of night is on my face
> Else would a maiden blush bepaint my cheek

it sounds thoroughly unlikely, quite apart from the fact that
she is in full studio lighting. She bends and gestures so hard,

through most of the scene, that there is no physical tension between love and modesty: only a wholly external contrast between being brassy and being arch. This scene is so bad, lacking all sense of pace and pitch, dissolving the very clear physical and verbal spacing which is at once dramatic and literary,
that the point of the subsequent scenes, in a different convention, is hopelessly compromised. Whatever else this may be, it
is not Shakespeare himself. It is not even a moderately competent twentieth century production.

And then back comes the compere. "Was there a boy called
Romeo Montagu?" he asks, looking us straight and friendly in
the practiced camera eye. It might even be nice to know, or
at least to have a program about that quite separate problem, if
the only alternative were the unholy mess so far. But it is only
introductory patter to the number of operatic treatments of
Shakespeare's play, and we fade to a scene from Gounod's
opera.

An extraordinary thing then happens. Partly by contrast
with the extreme ineptitude of the "Shakespeare himself" episode, and partly in its own terms, for reasons that we must examine, the scene immediately holds the attention. It is again
the unlocalized space of the television studio, though with more
imaginative lighting, and with a higher and better balcony and
better curtains. We suddenly realize the model for that first
balcony: a suburban porch, with Juliet having nowhere much
to go beyond the curtains, because they wouldn't be there anyway, and she knows it and is in and out like a flash. This opera
balcony looks like an opera balcony, and the gain is immediate.
But the biggest difference is in the delivery of the words. They
are now being sung, but, paradoxically (for this rarely happens in opera), they are consistently clearer and more audible
than in the spoken scene. The physical gestures which accompany them are the conventional gestures of the opera singer
and have a direct physical relation to the pace and rhythm. The
lovers again come to touch and make physical contact, but this
is done through simple conventional movements, particularly
of the hands.

It isn't Shakespeare, of course. It is Gounod's Shakespeare. But it is worth saying, as deliberately as one can, that the total effect of this operatic scene is much closer to the total effect of the written scene than was the first acted episode. It has often been observed that the methods of opera are dramatically closer to Shakespearean methods than are the methods of modern naturalist drama. The hand movements, in the touch over the balcony, are a simple version of the complicated and beautiful conventional touching in the first meeting of Juliet and Romeo, in Act One, Scene Five:

> If I profane with my unworthiest hand
> This holy shrine . .

That whole first meeting is a formal sonnet, in which the touch of hands and lips is a complicated pattern controlled by the words:

> And palm to palm is holy palmers' kiss . . .
> O then, dear saint, let lips do what hands do . . .

This method, at once more fluid and more extended in the balcony scene, is a world away from the calculation of probability in a meeting between young lovers. The emotions have been shaped into a clear artistic form which more perfectly expresses them than the probable inarticulacies of body and voice, and the more clearly this pattern is deliberately performed the more intense the dramatic emotion will be.

The scene from Gounod has its own form and conventions, controlled by the music, but in kind it belongs with Shakespeare. The form and rhythm of the scene are controlled, and there is also, one has to say, an available professionalism, in the highly trained singing, which makes the strongest possible contrast with the floundering amateurism of the acted episode. Indeed, the contrast of these two scenes is clear enough to be used as a basis for discussing the whole problem of convention in drama, and the particular problem of presenting Shakespeare in our own time. The operatic stage retains conventions and a

professionalism which are at least in the same world as Elizabethan drama. These are strong enough to be quickly recreated
in the television studio. The modern theater, with acting and
staging methods devised for quite different kinds of play, is
not only a long way from Shakespeare (a problem that has to
be faced in its own terms), but it is also not firm or clear
enough to carry itself over into the quite different physical environment of television. One's mind keeps going back to that
first acted episode and wondering again what on earth it was.
Not Shakespeare himself, or the Elizabethan theater, we have
already agreed. But then not the modern theater either, and,
perhaps most damningly, not television. For it would not be
impossible, given the nature of the television camera, to re-
create forms of speaking and movement which, based on altera-
tions and contrasts of angle, and a full use of close-ups, could
retain the clear dramatic form of the written scene. What we
get in the operatic scene is, in style, a television excerpt from
an operatic performance—and that is probably right, because
of the firm conventions of the operatic stage and the difficulties
of close-ups of operatic singers. What we get in the acted scene
is, paradoxically, not even in style a television excerpt from a
theatrical performance, where the stage would at least give
some shape, but a television excerpt from bad television: a
kind of infinite regress of failure.

But now the compere is back. We have become used to him,
and anyway we are well into the program and he doesn't have
to sell it so soft; he can even confine himself to what we are going to see. The ballet promises to be interesting, while we have
in our minds the questions about physical movement raised by
the two previous scenes. But this is to be a ballet of the whole
play, its speed apparently depending on the concentration
which formalized movement allows. For all this concentration,
we notice, the compere feels it necessary to explain one of the
movements: the hand across the face which covers it from the
object of its grief—in fact, I would have thought, a clear and
self-evident movement, but explained as "Juliet wanting to get
rid of her troubles."

It is a pity that the ballet, when it comes, is little more than mediocre. There could have been several better examples, in which we might have seen more clearly what formal expressive movement can do to embody this emotional pattern without the aid of words. The Tchaikowski music is itself highly expressive and, as it turns out, carries the ballet, rather than creating it. There is again the problem of convention, because the choreography is post-classical, yet on a familiar classical theme. There is incidental success, but the dancing is limited by a costuming which seems to come straight out of some naturalist habit of mind. Juliet begins in a sort of ball dress which makes almost all the leg movements inexpressive and then moves to what I suppose is a short nightdress (for it is nothing else that I know) for the balcony scene. The point here is that Juliet is dressed for the balcony setting of the stage play rather than for ballet. This severely limits the expressive possibilities of the dance and makes it less than a fair test and example. It is worth noting, however, that at certain points—notably the deaths— the power of dance movement is evident. It should also be noted that the lighting, which can be so crucial in television presentation, is more imaginatively used in this dance scene than in any of the other scenes. Romeo is separated from Juliet, for example, by the simple but very effective device of stepping out of the brilliantly lighted dancing circle. The camera mobility is not equally imaginative, though there are glimpses of what might have been done.

And so back to the compere and to *West Side Story*, which one feels the program has been waiting for. All right, there are the similarities of situation which he explains, but what we gain by seeing Tony and Maria in the Romeo and Juliet context is not clear. If it is just reminiscence, of the balcony scene and so on, it is unimportant and even distracting. We have in any case to see *West Side Story* as itself and not as another thing. The whole material is transformed, and then the isolation of the balcony scene is misleading. But what one realizes, watching it, is that this is what the producer would have really liked to do with that first acted scene from Shakespeare. The tenement balcony and the fire escape ladder make more sense than that pseudo-Renaissance suburban porch, and the looks and touches of a modern romantic encounter go better with the words of this new song than with the words of Shakespeare which even after the treatment I have described were still in some way present. These West Side looks and gestures, familiar from a thousand cinema and television screens, belonged with these words as they could never belong with Shakespearean verse. *Tonight, tonight, the world is full of light*: I mean we know how to look singing words like that, with suns and moons all over the place. Only was that a boy called Romeo Montagu? Or Tony? Or who?

Screening Shakespeare

I have focused so far on this single television program: the Westinghouse *Romeos and Juliets*. It is clear that I do not think highly of it, as a television program, though I would repeat my earlier view that it would make an excellent basis for a discussion of dramatic conventions and of the problems and opportunities in presenting Shakespeare in our media. Because the acted episode there was so bad, I want to put into evidence a much more considerable performance: the recent George Schaefer film of *Macbeth* (distributed in U.K. by British Lion).

This production was very evidently professional, and considerable thought had been given to the ways of performing Shakespeare on a screen. And then, quite apart from this, the speaking of the verse was at least at the level of the best contemporary professional theaters, though with a few of its mannerisms which I will mention first to get them out of the way. Thus when Macbeth came down, having murdered Duncan, he did not say

> I have done the deed.

He said

> I have . . . I have done the deed.

This is simply importing into Shakespeare the kind of "character" writing—"he can't quite bring himself to say it"—which a contemporary dramatist might feel necessary. Or again, Lady Macbeth did not say

> I'll gild the faces of the grooms withal
> For it must seem their guilt.

She said

> I'll gild the faces of the grooms withal
> For it
> Must
> Seem their guilt

This again is replacing the Shakespearean form with a different speech convention: acting rather than speaking the sense.

Yet, on the whole, there were few of these blemishes: many less indeed than in the ordinary professional stage production. And it is worth underlining this point, because the prejudice of our high culture, and of our educational system, against visual forms has produced an absurd situation. Thus it is common for teachers and others who believe they respect Shakespeare to assume in advance that a film or television production is some sort of vulgarization, whereas a production in a theater, perhaps by some company with the word Shakespeare in its title, is the real thing. But in fact most of the things that go wrong in filming or televising Shakespeare go equally wrong on the most distinguished stages. And why should they not, since they are usually done by the same people? Neither a film of a play by Shakespeare, nor a modern theater production, is particularly like a performance in an Elizabethan theater, which anyway we cannot recover. The only standard for either is the surviving text, and there is no built-in reason why this should not be performed as well on film or television as on a modern stage. The modern theater, that is to say, is also a modern medium; it is not, to use that convenient phrase again, "Shakespeare himself."

The central issue, on which I want to concentrate, is that of dramatic space. In a film production, or a television production using some film sequences, effects are possible which would be impossible on either an Elizabethan or modern stage. Thus, in the *Macbeth* under discussion, we can look at the castle of Dunsinane or at Birnam wood or at an army approaching across the moors. The addition of these scenes to the Shakespeare text seems to me quite unexceptionable. In so vigorous and active a form as Shakespearean drama, these additions fit well, and the opportunities they give for relevant spectacle (in film, of course, though rarely in television) seem to me usually to work with the play rather than against it. It would be unreasonably timid, having in any case abandoned the conventions of the Elizabethan theater, to forswear this kind of supporting effect. The whole thing could be dragged down to spectacle, certainly: yet another army appearing suddenly over that familiar western skyline. But in reasonable proportion, such sequences seem to me to add something wholly acceptable.

The real problem is their relation to the acted text. When they appear on their own, introductory or illustrative, they are convincing and lively. But the difficulty comes when they have to be matched with the spoken words. I will give some examples:

First, there are the speeches in which Shakespeare creates a powerful visual imagery. What, in a mobile visual form, ought then to be done?

Example One

> Light thickens, and the crow
> Makes wing to th' rooky wood.
> Good things of day begin to droop and drowse,
> Whiles night's black agents to their preys do rouse.

Sequence: Move from the close-up of Macbeth speaking to a longshot of the darkening hills, with moving shadows, as subdued rook cries are heard on the sound track.

The difficulty here is that the words are so powerful, and are
so known *in print*, that almost any visual accompaniment seems
superfluous. Yet, in any performance, we will be seeing something at this point, and this unemphatic use of a generalized
longshot and soundtrack seemed to serve as a wholly effective
background for the more particular images being created by
the words.

Example Two

> No jutty, frieze,
> Buttress, nor coign of vantage, but this bird
> Hath made his pendent bed and procreant cradle.

Sequence: Close-up of Banquo on horseback outside castle,
followed by brief longshot of castle walls.

This didn't work at all. Having established the castle, visually, as the Elizabethan stage would not, it seemed an odd ab-
stention from detail to have not the least suggestion of the
nests or the birds. With neither castle nor nests, the words
would have carried; with one but not the other, the words were
made to seem irrelevant and even evasive, a character comment on Banquo. Probably the director was scared of charges
to naivete (of the sort that probably came to mind when the
rook cries were mentioned in Example One) and settled for
the security of a genteel tact. But if you start a visual image
you have to go through with it; you can't switch conventions
in the middle.

Example Three

> And now a wood
> Comes toward Dunsinane . . .
> Now near enough. Your leafy screens throw down.

Sequence (selected): The boughs are seen being cut, in an
actual wood. In the castle, Macbeth is
told of the wood moving, and at the end

> of the scene rushes to the walls to look.
> A line of soldiers is carrying boughs. At
> the command they put them down.

This is quite wrong. The film could quite legitimately show Birnam wood moving, by the right kind of angled longshot; not the mechanics of the illusion, but the illusion itself. I found myself wanting, intensely, to see the wood move, in an emotion at that point wholly relevant to the real dramatic movement. To see the soldiers carrying branches is to jump back from the dramatic design to the accidental limits of stage technique.

Example Four

> Is this a dagger which I see before me?

Sequence: Macbeth is looking into a pseudo-fire. The flames rise just in front of the camera lens.

This, I suppose, is tact again, but one could also say that it is verbal cliché. Where does a man see pictures? Why, of course, in the fire. But the air-drawn dagger is quite natural film material, to which the words actually point. There is a problem of convention, in the matter of "supernatural" appearances, in the very text of *Macbeth*. The witches can be taken either way. In the film, their first appearance is in a misty hollow on the heath; their second appearance in the dream of the sleeping Macbeth, through whose head they appear by montage and back-projection. This device is defensible, as the "pictures in the fire" are not, because at least the witches do appear. But the dramatic problem of their metaphysical status—seers, agents of evil, or mere personal projection—is not to be solved by accidental variations of convention. We can also note here the sacking of Macduff's castle, in back-projection while Macbeth is speaking his intention. This is a technical device for compressing the play, and, however regrettable in that it in-

volves losing a written scene, is at least dramatically unambiguous.

Example Five

> My hands are of your colour; but I shame
> To wear a heart so white.

Sequence: The bloodstains on Macbeth's hands have already
been shown to us, from the moment he came down
the stair. When Lady Macbeth reenters, her bloodstained hands are again visible. But now, as she
comes towards him, there is a sudden close-up of
the hands of both. They meet, red with blood, and
are held for an instant. The slight delay, in close-up,
gives the impression of the hands stuck together by
blood.

It is common to criticize the use of blood (or red paint) on
cinema and television, and this use could easily be criticized as
sensational. But it seemed to me essentially right. The whole
visual convention, in this kind of film, demands that the blood
be shown. It is no more than this, no more than naturalism,
when we see the bloodstained hands of Macbeth or Lady Macbeth in medium-shot. Yet at the moment when the hands join,
and appear to stick together, there is not only an emphasis of
the bloodiness of the deed (an emphasis in itself quite simple
and ordinary) but also a visual enactment of the dramatic design: they are *held together* by the blood, as well as stained
and shamed by it. The most ordinary sensational cliché has
been transformed into an effective dramatic image.

The problem emerges, again and again, as one of visual convention and the nature of the playing-space. The most general
example, in the film as a whole, is the creation of the castle.
This is dramatically powerful, but it is not easy to maintain con-
sistency, within the dramatic design, between movements
around the castle and movements on and off the stage. The

created place can tie down the action as well as liberate and illustrate it. In general the castle settings are successful, but there is a bad lapse in the bedroom of Macbeth, which becomes suddenly an Italianate stage set, with balcony windows open to a blue sky and a Provençal pot on the window ledge, yet when with Macbeth we look beyond the ledge we see the bleak moors. This is not of course a tension between Shakespeare and the film, but between modern staging of Shakespeare and modern filming. It is hardly ever that the translation into film causes real difficulties. Where the film fails, it is because of incomplete translation. Behind this incompleteness, undoubtedly, lies the false prestige of the modern theatrical production as "Shakespeare himself." In this *Macbeth*, but much more in some other Shakespeare films, it is the fear of making a film without theatrical reminiscences that is creatively limiting. As with all conflicts between real art and respectable semiart, there can be many paradoxes.

A recent British commercial television production of *A Midsummer Night's Dream* tried to hang on to a large audience by engaging several well-known popular comedians to play Bottom and his fellow-mechanicals. The educated reaction to this was that it was a typical example of the vulgarization of Shakespeare. If some Shakespearean actors had been engaged, it would presumably have been good and dignified. In fact, the comedians did brilliantly, bringing professional *comic* techniques to scenes written for directly comparable talents. It was the first time in my experience that these scenes became genuinely funny in themselves. The difference from the customary genteel imitation of comedians was startling, and one remembered, in a genuine way, and not as the usual thought-stopping platitude, that Shakespeare wrote for a popular theater. Such successes, as yet, are small and scattered, but we need to remember them.

When we look, generally, at the contemporary relation between Shakespeare and the transmission of Shakespeare, we need to make finer discriminations than have so far been encouraged. We all have our stories of real vulgarization of

Shakespeare, as in some of the paper "illustrated classics" which reduce the plays to strip cartoons. These need as hard words as we can find. But the worst illusion of contemporary education is that over against such vulgarizations we can set "Shakespeare himself." What does this usually mean in practice? That we read the plays, often in school editions and for school purposes. But this, also, at its worst, is a travesty, and, at its best, still not "Shakespeare himself." The point is not only that the plays were written to be *acted*, though this is important enough. It is that they were conceived within a still predominantly oral culture and that much of their reality depends on this fact. Marshall McLuhan, in his controversial book *The Gutenberg Galaxy* (Toronto:. University of Toronto Press, 1962), has shown very clearly how a print culture, of the kind experienced between the seventeenth and early twentieth centuries, imposes its own medium-derived structures. The effects of this process on our understanding and teaching of Shakespeare are undoubtedly large, though they are mostly still unexplored. The printed text, above all, acquires a primary and isolated status, which can lead us to think that any performance is vulgarization: "Educated people, after all, can read it for themselves." And then, since high theater, within a print culture, was the only alternative we knew, "real" Shakespearean productions, which were in fact nineteenth or twentieth century versions of nineteenth or twentieth century readings of texts, were all we could envisage as performance.

It is clear, if we work on a Shakespearean text with performance in mind, taking our directions from the dramatic design actually embodied in the words, that the forms we have become used to, in the twentieth century theater, are as much an obstacle to our understanding as the critical commentaries on, say, characters, which were developed from habituation to novel reading. The problem of reading Shakespeare, to say nothing of performing him, is then a matter of breaking through these barriers, as far as we can, by an historical and critical awareness of their existence. We shall always fail to do this if we assume that the assumptions and habits of the last one or two generations are close to Shakespeare because they are "educated" and because they are in print. There has been, if you like, a high vulgarization as well as a low: making the plays into school reading texts is structurally comparable to making them into strip cartoons, though of course nobody doubts that the former retain more real content than the latter. What we now most need, however, in a culture in which the status of print as the major transmitter of art is no longer single and simple, is a fresh look at that most difficult question in all drama: the relation between text and performance. The trouble is that we think we know this: the text is what we read at school or university; the performance is what we see on a twentieth century stage. If we can get beyond this, to a more open situation, we shall have made a cultural advance, as opposed to a mere cultural adjustment. The filming and televising of Shakespeare that we have seen so far is very mixed in quality, but with more errors from old habits than from new experiments. It is at least possible to conceive that the flexibility of place, the mobility of viewpoint, the variation of imagery, which cinema and television make possible, will take us farther into an understanding of Shakespeare than the static theaters of a past generation. How we then see the problem is this: not to transmit, in some handy popular form, the "Shakespeare himself" who is somehow magically in our possession; but to know what we can, in our culture and through our own means of performance, of a body of art which as itself and as a whole is in any case not to be recovered. The new media are among our major tools for this substantial attempt, and we shall just have to put up with the jeers of those who think their Edwardian novelist or interwar poet is "Shakespeare himself." Paradoxically, as we fade those jeers out, we shall have to be all the tougher on the errors in our own kind of experiment.

Education and High Culture

It is the business of education to transmit a cultural tradition and to help us to understand our own world. In this task, the teacher of English has a central place, because he is concerned above everything else with our common language. And to think about language is to think about the relation between the tradition and the present. The language is our mother tongue, the experience of our own people, at the same time as it is also our most ordinary and everyday currency of feeling and business and thought. We can never separate out and contrast the "tradition" and "the present." The tradition exists only in so far as we make it present, and it is in any case always selective: we take from the past not its whole content but what we need for the present. And this is right and inevitable: only what is now living is available and significant.

But then how do we relate this way of looking at tradition to Matthew Arnold's famous definition of culture as "the best which has been thought and said in the world"? Many people interpret this definition as requiring a paramount loyalty to the best work of the past. English teachers, particularly, often see their duties in this way and go on to contrast the cultural values of the past with the cultural depravity of the present: the English teacher against "mass culture." But to anyone who sees the matter in this way, it is worth repeating what Arnold actually said. He defined his purpose as to

> recommend culture as the great help out of our present difficulties; culture being a pursuit of our total perfection by means of getting to know, on all the matters which most concern us, the best which has been thought and said in the world; and, through this knowledge, turning a stream of fresh and free thought upon our stock notions and habits.[1]

It is surely impossible to reduce this to an inert contrast of values between past and present, between "Shakespeare himself" and the vulgarities of cinema and television. Arnold's conception is a very active one, and it begins in the present, "on all the matters which most concern us." We take from the past, on these matters, "the best which has been thought and said in

---

[1] Preface to *Culture and Anarchy*.

the world," and *through* this knowledge, turn a stream of fresh and free thought on the notions and habits of our own world. This is not at all the contrast of tradition and the present; it is the selective use of the tradition to meet our present difficulties.

The worst way to preserve "high culture," by which we can mean the great art and thought of the past, is to seek to oppose it to the present. The logical error becomes a social and cultural error. It is true that great art and thought challenges not only inferior work but also the muddle and incompleteness of much ordinary experience. But it challenges those everywhere, in the past quite as much as in the present. It is not the past that we celebrate, in celebrating high culture, but the best of the past, which was also a challenge to the past, as it is still a challenge to the present. To cut off high culture, by intention or default, from this challenging relation to experience at any time is in fact to betray it. It lives by its constant and immediate relation to all our living. When, as in the cases we have been discussing, we see the work of Shakespeare in tension with the cinema and television of our own time, we see it in its inevitable relation. The history of our experience of Shakespeare, through three and a half centuries, is a history of many kinds of this very tension. Consider Shakespeare in the Restoration theater, being rewritten and revised; in the eighteenth century theater, being adapted to a bourgeois sensibility; in the nineteenth century theater, being loaded with archaeological productions; in nineteenth and twentieth century thought, being used as an instance for our own inquiries and explanations. In every one of these cases, something of "Shakespeare himself" has quite certainly been lost, to say nothing of the many obvious additions. But the process as a whole is inevitable, and the best we can do, at any time, is to realize that it is happening and is bound to happen, and then bring all the intelligence and sensibility we can to bear on the *details* of the process. We are never without some independent check; we can read the works, and study their context, and get as near as we can to "Shakespeare himself." But Shakespeare now will always be touched by the present; our business is to see that this relationship is as creative, as deep, as imaginatively true as we can make it. And this needs constant experiment, which, as I have already argued, is least likely to be fruitful if some immediate past phase of the understanding of Shakespeare is taken as absolute.

The point is very general, and I will give two further considerations. We do not need to be told how much of the culture of our own time is inadequate and even degraded. But we must be very careful not to use "low culture" or "mass culture" in different senses at once. There is inadequate or degraded work, now often distributed in great quantity. There is unfamiliar work, in new forms both popular and unpopular, from abstract art to jazz. And there is, in any case, a new and much larger audience, called by some for political reasons, "the masses": a term of contempt which has taken over from mob. Now which of these different things is *mass culture*? The degraded work? But there is degraded work also in contemporary high culture, and indeed there has rarely been a time in which the themes and methods of "high art" and "mass art" have been closer; think, for example, of contemporary artistic uses of violence. Is it the large audience then? Some people would have us think so. But such an attitude is only part of the powerful conservative reaction to the growth of democracy: the trained reflex that other people, "in the mass," are inevitably vulgar. No teacher at least can believe this, or he is in the wrong job. If the argument is right, it would be better to close down all the schools, except a few class or elite institutions. Or is "mass culture" the unfamiliar work, found in the new media and using new conventions? The attitude of many people to cinema and television suggests that this is so, though the same people would regard such an attitude as philistine if applied to abstract art or the stream-of-consciousness novel. "Low equals unfamiliar" is one of the great cultural traps. The popular Elizabethan drama itself was regarded, by some traditionalists, as "low" in its own time. The novel in the eighteenth century was regarded as a "low" form. And in fact, in each of these cases, much of the work was ephemeral; some of it inadequate and degraded. But, shaped in its time, the new form was also the medium for the most important new and creative work. To defend a *form* as traditionally "high" is absurd. What as teachers we have to defend is the practice of excellence, and the procedures of detecting and describing badness, and if we are really to do this we cannot afford to start with "stock notions and habits." I teach in a college which was founded in the fifteenth century, and some of the buildings are even older. But I know that the spirit of the college, as it is now understood, is very recent and of our own century (though, often, I think, not quite enough of our century). I enjoy the tension between this embodied spirit and the strictly contemporary pressures and demands: there is good and bad on both sides, and out of the tension value will come. But I get really angry when somebody tries to pass off the spirit of the fifteenth century as age-hallowed; like most other "age-old traditions," like the ordinary version of "Shakespeare himself," it was quite recently invented, taking what it wanted from the tradition and dropping the rest. That is the way of institutions, but when we have an actual body of work which can be looked at freshly in each generation and which always to some extent survives in its own terms, the challenge is much harder.

The question is sometimes put: Should we try to pass on "high culture," such as the work of Shakespeare, to the new cultural generations and classes, or should we rather encourage a new high culture in the media of our own time? The answer, as I see it, is that to do either well is to create the conditions for both. Like every generation before us, we have to read and perform Shakespeare as well as we can in our own circumstances and through our own forms of communication. Whenever this is really attempted—I mean when it is accepted as a creative challenge and not as a prestige operation or a traditional routine—the response is encouraging. But the attempt meets much the same obstacles as the attempt to do new creative work. Education authorities have bought some standard annotated edition of a Shakespeare play; they have no money or no time, they say, to pay for making or seeing a Shakespeare film. As for art generally, they have the past in their storerooms; new art would be risky. That is what is called a defense of tradition and high culture: a betrayal of what the activities really are. Tradition, for these authorities, plays the role that profit plays in the general cultural apparatus. The business men who control so much of our cultural production and distribution also have their established works: the routines and formulas they know the public will buy; anything else would be risky. The contemporary artist, as creator or interpreter, has to struggle against both these worlds—most of his life. Is it not time for the teacher, unequivocally, to join him?

Charles Winick
Mariann P. Winick

Television and the Culture of the Child: *Exploring* on the Renaissance

The lore and language of children reflect their television viewing; the whole children's culture of our time is touched by the medium in many ways. Television meets the curiosity of young people on many levels. One such level is represented by a television series for children that is entertaining yet enlightening, and facilitates but does not force learning: *Exploring*. By examining the series and specifically its "Lorenzo de Medici" program, it is possible to obtain clues, not only to children's programs but also to other aspects of the child's life.

Exploring, although entirely original in conception, illustrates some of the qualities found in other successful series for children. It has a permanent host, as does *Captain Kangaroo*. It uses puppets somewhat like *Kukla, Fran and Ollie*, a puppet program that tapped elements of curiosity and character by its wide range of personalities and the scope of the contemporary situations with which it dealt. *Exploring* presents science in terms of principles and functional experiments like *Mr. Wizard*, the host of which performs experiments and discusses their significance and interpretation. It uses folk material and is shown in color, like *The Wonderful World of Color*, in which Walt Disney presents folk and historical materials in dramatic form.

Exploring is a weekly one hour program in color that began in 1962 and is shown midday Saturday. Its permanent host is

137

scientist Dr. Albert Hibbs. During its first year, the opening half hour examined language, music, and mathematics, and was geared to the younger members of the 5-12 age range. The second half hour, devoted to social studies and science, was primarily for older children. It dropped the mathematics segment after the first year. The five content themes of the program were established curriculum areas in the elementary school.

Two different puppet groups were members of the original cast, but only one has remained. That the program's regular cast does not include children probably helps it to attract a child audience since the presentation of a child on screen may pose problems in projection and identification for a youthful audience. Craig Fisher, the first producer of the NBC series, was largely responsible for its format and style.

Storytelling is the principal tool of the language section, with backgrounds including stylized animation, music, and sound. The stories fall into three categories: folk tales, mythology, and the meanings of words. Starting a program with a story is an almost ideal way to arouse interest in all age groups, since storytelling is one of the oldest art forms. One asset of the series is its regular use of celebrities from the entertainment world whose reputation is likely to be known, especially to the parents. Such celebrities were frequently used in the language section. The speech and diction of some, e.g., Cyril Ritchard, are so excellent that many parents are delighted to have their children listen to them.

The music portion alternates among dance performances, musical artists, and presentation of instruments. The mathematics segment emphasized concepts rather than numbers, by puppets and animation. Social studies are presented by music, dancing, film, and animation. The science segment is centered on live, taped, and filmed experiments. Appeal is maximized when the program is fun to watch. The puppets in the mathematics segments represented an arresting format for material that is traditionally difficult to present. The use of animal puppets to convey mathematics, for example, is a minimally "academic" approach.

Television for children above the nursery years has tended to compartmentalize its offerings, much as education does. Children enjoy and can profit from thinking in terms of relationships, similarities, and incongruities. Their verifications can continually lead to new verifications. *Exploring* is one of the few programs that has sought to present the Gestalt process rather than the fractionation of the subject matter. Its Gestalt approach has helped to make its presentations provocative rather than pedantic. Among the features that build interest in the program is that each one has a central theme, so that relationships among a variety of subjects can be suggested. During its first year, the theme of every program was a thing; during the second, the theme was a person, either historical or contemporary.

The broadcast time is an important factor in determining the size and level of attention of its audience. Just as the composition of the theater audience for a Wednesday matinee is likely to be quite different from that for a Saturday evening performance, and just as each is likely to have differing expectations of the performance, children in the television audience are likely to have a different "set" at different hours and days. *Exploring* follows three hours of entertainment programs consisting of cartoons, puppets, filmed shows about pet animals, and "action adventure" staples like the *Mounted Police*. Such programs are standard Saturday morning fare. Saturday afternoon is usually devoted to adult cultural programs, frequently unsponsored, dealing with the arts, education, and similar subjects. The timing of the program would therefore seem to maximize its role as a bridge between entertainment and seriousness. The period from one to two p.m. is transitional in terms of the day and is the lunch hour in many homes. Saturday may not be the ideal day for such a program because of its being traditionally the child's day for fun in contrast to Sunday, which is more solemn and family oriented.

The audience for *Exploring* has remained fairly constant. During the 1963-64 season in which the "Lorenzo de Medici" episode appeared, *Exploring* averaged an audience of 18 percent of all the sets in use at the time. During this hour an average of 22.7 percent of the sets were tuned in, so that the program's 18 percent of 22.7 percent gave it an audience of 2,100,000 homes. These homes had 3,900,000 viewers, of whom there were 900,000 men, 1,000,000 women, 300,000 teenage children, and 1,700,000 children under 12, with a concentration from 9 to 12, although some were as young as 4. This audience can be instructively compared with that for a typical Saturday morning children's cartoon program, *Mighty Mouse Playhouse*, at 10: 30. It has an audience of 40 percent of the 25.6 percent of the sets in use during the hour, or 5,340,000 homes and 10,600,000 viewers, consisting of 400,000 men, 600,000 women, 1,300,000 teenagers, and 8,300,000 children under 12. The cartoon program has many more viewers, but a much smaller proportion of adults. It is likely that many of the adults watching *Exploring* were doing so as one way of keeping up with their children's learning. The proportion of adults watching *Exploring* is greater than that watching any other children's program.

The goal of *Exploring* is not to teach but to excite and interest the child to go to his teacher or to a reference book in order to get more information. Its audience seems to consist more of inquisitive than of bright children, and audience research confirms that the bright child does not watch the program more than the average child. That the audience is inquisitive was suggested by one research finding that 40 percent of the viewers of a representative program had tried to get more information about something seen on it. Another clue is that mail from both children and adults tends to increase when a subject is presented relatively incompletely. Such mail typically asks for more information about the subject.

Although the host is a "Dr.," he is relaxed and friendly rather than authoritarian and thus probably minimally disturbing to children. Many children who may not be clear on just what his doctorate means may regard him as a kind of authority figure without portfolio. Dr. Hibbs facilitates the shift from one subject to another by appropriate introductory remarks.

A Teacher's Guide for the program is mailed generally every

three weeks to more than 260,000 elementary school teachers, representing over one third of the teachers who have classes with students in the target age group. It gives a synopsis of the program and suggests various class activities. It also raises some areas for further discussion in class and cites book and other relevant materials. The Teacher's Guide is explicit in making recommendations on the next step that boys and girls could take in further exploration of a given subject. It presents many questions, of a kind that could be asked by both student and teacher.

The "Lorenzo de Medici" program, shown on December 14, 1963, presented various facets of the Renaissance. Lorenzo was the focus because he was the personification of so many different aspects of that period. In order to heighten continuity and movement, the program was not broken into the traditional subject matter segments and the usual set was not employed. By elimination of the standard set, Dr. Hibbs might have a more integrated and three-dimensional role rather than being outside the action and commenting on it.

Dr. Hibbs opened the program by welcoming the audience to Renaissance Florence and introducing an animated Italian folk story about the Florentine traveler, Ansaldo, who had given two cats to a Canary Island town so that the town could fight its rats. The townfolk gave Ansaldo many gifts in gratitude. His friend Giocondo was excited by Ansaldo's story and visited the same town, bringing many valuables. Giocondo expected treasures in return, and the townfolk gave him their most precious possession: two cats. The story, "The Most Precious Possession," narrated by former Hit Parade singer Dorothy Collins, was told by photographic animation of several hundred pictures painted in Italy for the program. As the narrator spoke, camera movement and sound effects infused life into the pictures.

However, the theme of the story was not central to the theme of Florence in the Renaissance, nor was a woman narrator entirely consonant with a program devoted to the Renaissance, which was so preeminently characterized by men.

The music portion included six musicians playing carnival music, dance music ("La Magdelena"), a song written by Lorenzo, and one for which he wrote the lyrics. The segment might have been given more kinetic interest if time had permitted the dance itself to be shown, or if English subtitles had been flashed on the screen for songs as they were being sung. The musical instruments were those actually used at court. A man and woman shown singing to each other probably helped to improve identification of both sexes. One goal of this segment was to convey a feeling of how the music of the Renaissance sounded and how the instruments looked.

Although another point of this charming segment was that many a singer tried to trick his accompanist, the point was probably too recondite for many young viewers. The music segment was very sophisticated, but a child interested in music might be able to get much from it. In other programs, it was likely that a child might similarly be excited by only one segment although finding the others of some interest.

The third section primarily sought to communicate the meaning of perspective in art and used the program's regular puppets. One of the puppets is painting portraits and explains what she is doing to another puppet. Dr. Hibbs talks to them and discusses some famous paintings of the period, as well as some of the techniques of the painters of the Renaissance. He cites their role in the introduction of perspective in art. One of the puppets paints a portrait of Hibbs, who closes the segment with further remarks on Renaissance artists. If time had permitted, actually showing how paints are mixed would have been very exciting to children, especially in color. One of the most interesting parts of the 1959 exhibit on "How To Look at a Painting" of the Junior Museum of the Metropolitan Museum of Art was its presentation of how to mix paints and create colors. The Daliesque ending of the segment, with Mona Lisa smiling, may have been designed to interest adult viewers. However, it may have puzzled a number of young viewers, to whom its relevance to the Renaissance may not have been apparent.

The last segment combined science, art, and social studies.

It opened with Dr. Hibbs discussing the activities of the Medici family, followed by a film on Florentine sculpture and another on the changes in society during the fourteenth century. The film on social change, as well as the introductory story, had a kinetic quality that matched that of the program's signature, which consists of a boy running, a child's drawing of the sun, and a paperfolded boat sailing on water.

A film on Renaissance architecture followed a discussion of Michelangelo. Discussing the architecture, Dr. Hibbs introduced the subject of Leonardo da Vinci and his inventions. He presented models of da Vinci's inventions, but too briefly to permit relating them visually to their contemporary developments like the helicopter. Dr. Hibbs concluded with a brief summary after a film on Renaissance art.

The final scene, with Dr. Hibbs turning and walking slowly through the group of courtiers, probably helped to remind the audience of what had happened earlier and to reinforce Dr. Hibbs' role. The extensive presentation of Renaissance art and architecture was developed from existing still or motion picture photography that had been selected and edited. After the writer had prepared the script, he and the director selected appropriate film footage. The color provided texture and richness that was especially appropriate to the Renaissance, although of course it could not be seen on the great majority of sets that are black and white.

The second half of the program provided a rhythm and flow that were absent from the more static first half. The direction in the second half was clearly demonstrative while in the first half it was more descriptive. This may have partially reflected the first half's being geared toward the young child, while the art and architecture content of the second half facilitated a more interesting pace and aesthetic experience. The art and architecture aspects of the Renaissance, because they are visual, are also more likely to be familiar to children than the period's folklore or music. Content areas that are known to be of interest to boys and girls help to sustain their interest in a program.

The good taste that permeated the whole program can be inferred from its having shown Michelangelo's sculpture of the nude David without one letter of protest having been received, although such a scene on a children's program would ordinarily have elicited much protest. In the same segment it may have been the unavailability of appropriate film footage that led to the showing of Michelangelo's sculpture "La Notte," from the Medici Chapel in Florence, rather than to his magnificent sculpture of Lorenzo, which is only a few feet away in the very same room as "La Notte." If this had been a program for adults during evening hours, its budget would doubtless have been large enough to permit sending a camera crew to Florence to take photographs of such material. But even a program like *Exploring*, which probably has a larger budget than any other children's series, apparently cannot afford location planning.

In the limited time available, "Lorenzo de Medici" gave an overview of the Renaissance that touched on many aspects of the period. Relating each segment to Lorenzo, through the person of the narrator, provided continuity for a vast theme.

The "Lorenzo de Medici" program represented the usual level of the *Exploring* series, which is far more thoughtful and ambitious and aware of the needs of children than most programs for children are. A program which neglected the special requirements of the child audience was one devoted to fairy tales and hosted by Shirley Temple (*Shirley Temple Storybook*), which would seem to have been an ideal combination. But the series was not really written for children; the scripts did not convey the wonder of fairy tales, and it never attracted a substantial audience.

Entertainment programs for children are likely to be concerned primarily with keeping the child in front of the set and establishing as large an audience as possible. Almost all network children's programing is conceived, written, and presented without any consideration of how it relates to what children are learning in school. *Exploring* is one of the rare network entertainment programs that relate program content to curriculum in an interesting way. Any evaluation of the series must be made in the light of its pioneering status and the lack of previous models. The only other children's series with similar goals is *Discovery* (ABC), which is less ambitious, a half hour long, and is devoted completely to one subject each program. *Reading Room* (CBS) was a half hour series devoted to books.

One reason for the comparative dearth of interesting network series for young people is that a relatively exciting style is needed to win a young audience in a noncaptive situation. Many locally developed programs for children have managed, on a modest scale, to find such an exciting style.[1] Working on only a fraction of the budget of a network series, such local programs can reach only a very small proportion of a network's audience.

Television and the Child

Data from the field of child development lend themselves to generalizations about how television stimulates the curiosity of children. General propositions about young viewers can help teachers who work with programs like *Exploring*. Such statements must consider that the traditional approaches in the criticism of movies, perhaps the most similar other medium, are not really relevant because of a number of technical characteristics of television. Unlike films, television has a relatively limited ability to make use of contrasts in lighting or to use long shots very extensively. Some general observations can, however, suggest how the medium touches the lives of young people.

Television is less likely to appeal to children merely because it is available than it is to do so because it meets the overwhelming needs of children for stimulation via seeing and hearing. Seeing and hearing are central because education today presumes prior experience with them as a basis for classroom learning. The whole educational process still is based primarily

[1] Ralph Garry, F. B. Rainsberry, and Charles Winick, *For the Young Viewer* (New York: McGraw-Hill Book Co., 1962).

on the eye and ear, in spite of the prophetic urgings of Maria Montessori a half century ago that it was necessary to assist children in moving along all the sensory developmental tracks.[2]

Television is so important a visual stimulus because it feeds the child's interest in oral incorporation and provides him with both an ongoing relationship and a repetitive pattern. A child can comprehend situations on television far more easily than in daily activities because the medium makes it relatively easy for him to know what will happen next. A child of eight can develop an awareness of when the climax of a program will come and of how the climax will be resolved. In a half hour program there is a limited number of characters, their activities are circumscribed, and the activities stem from their roles. The visual cues communicated in a half hour program are explicit, even though the range of what is communicated may be less than can be acquired in a half hour of reading. Television is far more likely to show close-ups than movies, thus providing the child with an opportunity to see the appearance and functions of objects and faces with a detail and clarity that is otherwise impossible.

From the child's point of view, the most important aspect of television is that it is not only visual but also kinetic: an active image on the screen. The image's being smaller than life reinforces the child's desire to continue to return to it because he feels able to control it much more easily than he can the large picture on the movie screen. This fantasy experience of mastery has a counterpart in reality in the child's ability to change a television program by flicking a knob.

The "vision" in television is especially significant because seeing has become the most typical sensory modality of children, and indeed of adults, since the Industrial Revolution. Dimensions like touch, texture, size, and weight have lost much of their previous importance. A child who once would have used his knowledge of such dimensions in opening a door latch

---

[2] Maria Montessori, *The Discovery of the Child* (Madras, India: Kalakshetra Publications, 1948).

can open a contemporary door by simply touching his palm to its surface and pushing. The latch gave way to the knob, and the knob yielded to the knobless door. Not only have doors changed so radically that a latch is now a rarity, but the proportion of doors in the home has declined. As a result of many such technological changes, of which the door is only a small example, the development of tactile sensitivity and of the wrist and hand is far more retarded in the child of today than in his predecessor. In one recent study of the self references of young children, they were relatively unable to focus attention on their limbs but tended to identify themselves with their torsos.[3] Several other kinds of evidence suggest that the child of today tends to be less and less likely to identify with specific parts of the body.[4] The use of sensory modalities other than eye and ear has been steadily diminishing.

Television also stimulates children's curiosity by its strong appeal to hearing. The clarity with which it transmits sound is far greater than in ordinary discourse, even than in the classroom. Many a teacher is not a paradigm of good or interesting speech; and one of the less fortunate aspects of educational television is that so many of its lecturers are teachers whose speech is poor.

Because children respond favorably to precision in speech, television helps stimulate their interest in words and language. *Exploring* is an example of a program that provides a model of good speech without talking down to children. It can provide a broader range of vocabulary and good patterns of language use. *Exploring* generally makes the meaning of new words or concepts as clear as possible as soon as they are introduced. Sometimes when children hear an unfamiliar word, their stopping to ponder its meaning causes them to lose the gist of what follows.

---

[3] Mariann P. Winick, "Verbal and Non-verbal Self References in Children" (Ph.D. Dissertation, New York University, 1964).

[4] Seymour Fisher and Sidney E. Cleveland, *Body Image and Personality* (Princeton: D. Van Nostrand Co., 1958).

Television exercises another modality of hearing. A major loss in our society has been the substitution of noise for sound. Urban children never learn to distinguish the sounds of an activity like birds' singing. In addition, the traditional rhythms of nonurban life are as absent today as they are from the music of contemporary composers like John Cage. Children, especially young children, need to respond to sound on the level of rhythms that they can duplicate. But it is hard to duplicate the rhythms of a Shostakovich, as compared with those of a Brahms or of a folk song. Rhythm, rather than words, is the basic ingredient in nursery rhymes like Mother Goose. Rhythm is also the central ingredient in children's street chants, which appear to have an almost universal tempo that suggests that, at least in Western civilization, there are some paths of order in children's response to sound that transcend national boundaries.[5]

Television's stress on rhythm meets many of these same basic needs—by the sound of commercials, program signatures, musical auditory cues like those for excitement, the repetitive rhythms and semiabstract qualities of cartoons. The child who will be able to say "Be My Ballantine" but who cannot explain its meaning is merely demonstrating that the rhythmic feeling of syllables is more important to him than the meaning of the words. Perhaps the extraordinary popularity of rock-and-roll music among young people is a regression, during preadolescence and adolescence, to a Mother Goose level of auditory satisfaction. It may occur because a kind of sensory homeostasis operates to reinforce the auditory sense at a time when the other senses are so undeveloped.

Television thus uniquely feeds the curiosity of the senses for visual stimuli, words, and sound. This meeting of children's needs for basic sensory experiences is central in any attempt to explain what children do with the medium. Many of the content analyses and other quasi-literary studies of television programs for children deal with a secondary and far less important

---

[5] Iona Opie and Peter Opie, *The Love and Language of Schoolchildren* (Oxford: Oxford University Press, 1960).

level of satisfaction than the primary sensory modalities by which the medium communicates to children.

The medium also stimulates by its ability to generate inner speech. Rather than being a one-way communicator, it may create conditions for an interior dialogue far more favorable than are possible in other situations. Vygotsky has suggested that verbal speech is less important in the development of thought than inner speech, and Montessori observed that by concentrating and not talking, a child may be doing something more important than talking. [6, 7] Some programs for preschoolers are valuable for the audience that they provide the young viewer. Such programs may provide the child with a chance to talk or sing or clap or otherwise imitate in psychologically healthy ways. Preschoolers respond to rhythms and the use of instruments like clappers or tambourines, with their repetitive patterns.[8] The Beatles appeal to children in so many cultures not only because of their amalgam of bisexuality and masturbatory handling of their instruments, but primarily because their rhythm is clear and regular. The lyrics to their songs hardly matter, except insofar as they consist of repetitive phrases.

It is possible to identify specific ways in which television stimulates specific age groups. We can classify such groups as the preschool (3-5), juvenile (6-9), preadolescence (10-12), and adolescence (13 +). For the purpose of illustration we can consider one dimension of children's personality (humor), television coverage of a specific event (an election), and one series format (western).

Each of the developmental levels of youth can stimulate its sense of humor by television. The preschooler learns to laugh at pantomimic action, as in programs like the *Three Stooges.*

---

[6] Lev S. Vygotsky, *Thought and Language* (New York: John Wiley and M.I.T. Press, 1962).

[7] Maria Montessori, *The Absorbent Mind* (Madras, India: Theosophical Publishing House, 1949).

[8] Charles Winick, "The World of the Young Viewer," in Ralph Garry, F. B. Rainsberry, and Charles Winick, *For the Young Viewer* (New York: McGraw-Hill Book Co., 1962), pp. 143-177.

Many a juvenile enjoys laughing at the ridiculous actions of adults in situation comedies whose antics have an effect similar to nonsense verse. Preadolescents respond to spoofs of adult institutions via parody or satire, as in programs like *Car 54, Where Are You?* and *The Munsters*. Adolescents are among the most loyal fans of television comedians, often to get jokes for their own social activities.

The interest of young people in a national event like an election may help to stimulate their subsequent role as citizens. Preschoolers know about candidates and parties, primarily through television which permits them to learn about the workings of representative government far earlier than previous generations did. The juvenile becomes actively involved in the competition between the candidates and identifies with them. Since the television age, preadolescents have been handing out campaign buttons, and even doing errands at political party offices. Their discussions of campaign issues among themselves largely derive from their interest in news programs about the election. The adolescent, whose whole world involves comparative judgments, tends to use television coverage of elections as a springboard to studying how other media handle the event.

Another heuristic approach to the study of the relationship of young people to television is provided by aesthetics. Probably the most lasting single format of the medium is the western, and one major aspect of its popularity among young people is sensori-aesthetic.[9] For the preschooler, the physical beauty of a man riding a horse, in a context that draws on the romantic past, has a profound psychological appeal. Preschoolers love to trot, gallop, and imitate riding a horse, and to have the aesthetic experience of bodily movements that are not available in their ordinary walking and running. For the juvenile, a western environment with its unusual characters and costumes exerts a great hold over fantasy. The myth of the West and the fron-

---

[9] Charles Winick and Mariann P. Winick, "Some Uses of Home Television Viewing in the Elementary Classroom," *Childhood Education Membership Service Bulletin 9-A, Homework—The Home's Part, The School's Part* (1963-64), pp. 27-39.

tier, especially for children whose ancestors came from other countries, is exciting and inspires much of their own painting and drawing.

For the preadolescent, the perceptual experience of a complex amalgam of words and actions is itself aesthetic. Experiencing the auditory and visual cues that permit a child to follow the relationships among hero, villain, and environment can be as aesthetically revealing and satisfying as an older person's response to a sophisticated drama. The adolescent is ready to utilize his viewing of television westerns in order to make qualitative comparisons with other types of dramatic programs and with the representation of westerns in other media.[10]

The Child Culture

Television programs, like *Exploring*, specifically designed for appeal to children are only the most recent facets of the whole movement that has characterized our "century of the child." The trend toward material specifically for children is one that began with the Industrial Revolution, when children's participation in factory work accelerated so fast that reformers became concerned about it. If children's place was not in the factory, where was it? One obvious answer was that more children belonged in school, and what happened in school began getting attention. Reformers like Froebel, Dewey, and Montessori stressed the unique significance of the child as father of the man, rather than as a little man.

The stress on the role of childhood led to emphasis on prenatal and maternal care and the development of medical specialties for each of these fields. Child development became an established discipline, with its own centers and an apparatus of professional societies and journals. Special clothing and foods for the infant, the teething child, and the toddler became household necessities.

---

[10] Charles Winick, "Children's Television Fan Mail," *Television Quarterly*, 3 (1964), 57-71.

World War II was a benchmark in these changes. It created a situation in which many children were forced to live away from their parents and facilitated opportunities for exploring the effects of special environments on children. With the anticipated postwar increase in births, many aspects of the economy could and did prepare products specifically for children. The enormous postwar interest in psychiatry and especially in psychoanalysis made Freud's views on the nature of childhood common household currency. One partial result of the great influence of Freud was the desire of many families to give each child his own room, previously a prerogative of the wealthy. The decreasing size of the family made it easier to organize such living arrangements, as did the decrease in the number of grandparents living with their children. Frank Lloyd Wright could never understand the "mysterious reason" for which boys and girls must be separated in American homes.[11]

A specific children's culture has been developing on many different levels. Museums for children made their first appearance.[12] Films for children, largely inspired by Walt Disney's creation of characters like Donald Duck and Mickey Mouse, become big business. Toys are created specifically for children and are no longer small editions of adult material. Children's art, humor, and games seem to be similar in many parts of Western civilization.

Programing for children began with radio, with the early evening hours studded with programs like *Let's Pretend, The Lone Ranger*, and the *Singing Lady*. Phonograph records for children were a novelty even a generation ago. Today they are commonplace. The children's book market has expanded because such books tend to be bought by parents whose belief that a book is the safest gift for a child echoes our society's stress on literacy and sedentary activity for children. The number of books for children has mushroomed since World

---

[11] Frank Lloyd Wright, *The Natural House* (New York: Mentor Books, 1963), pp. 165–166.

[12] Charles Winick, "The Public Image of the Museum in America," *Curator* 5 (1962), 45–52.

War II and now comes to over 2,700 new titles each year. Their quality has increased steadily since the 1930's as one result of the influence of prizes for excellence in children's books, like the Newbery Award. Since the 1950's, their quality and format have also improved as one way of competing with television.

An analogy can be drawn between the level of interest of children in specific kinds of literature and in types of television programs. The reader of comic and picture books is likely to enjoy television cartoons. The fan of western stories and novels will probably respond to western and adventure stories on the 21″ screen. Followers of serial books like Nancy Drew and the Bobbsey Twins should be ready to follow the many family situation comedies on television. Readers of animal books can find their friends like Fury and Lassie on programs that combine a family with a pet or nature appeal, which is also the combination of literary favorites like *Swiss Family Robinson* and *Black Beauty*. Programs that are linked to books provide a new dimension for comparative criticism.

The almost implacable television requirement of a weekly format means that there is either a continuity of character or of format. Such continuity makes television programs more likely to provide satisfactions similar to those of the movie serials of the 1930's, or to book series like *Tom Swift*, than to the satisfactions of nonseries books like *Island of the Blue Dolphin* or *The Three Policemen*. Occasionally "spectaculars" for children, like "Quillow and the Giant," invite comparison with some of the best nonseries books.

Perhaps the most intense development of a children's culture has occurred over the last fifteen years in the flowering of an explicitly teen culture. There are now over twenty magazines specifically for teenagers, in addition to the few magazines from the past that are intended for either boys or girls. Singers like Fabian, Connie Francis, and Paul Anka became millionaires entirely on the basis of their teen followings. The teen group is the only one which has been increasing its movie-going, and many films are made specifically for this market, which has increased from 15 to 20 million in the last generation. Teenagers feel so secure about their relationship to the adult world that their magazine of satire of adult mores, *Mad*, has the largest newsstand circulation in the country.[13] Teens have developed their own jokes and other humor. One reason that their culture has assumed such powerful dimensions is that they have over ten billion dollars a year to spend, and many media and other groups help to teach them how to spend this money.

Because the hold of popular media like movies, television, and phonograph records on teens and other young people is so great, these media deserve the most careful criticism. Teachers can be especially helpful in guiding their students to distinguish publicity from criticism and to apply appropriate values to the popular arts. A program or performer who is widely publicized may not be very talented, and the teacher can help the student to distinguish the gold of talent from the dross of publicity. Since the viewing of television is likely to be the most important later leisure activity of the student, the contribution of the teacher to his student's post-graduation life can be substantial to the extent that the teacher is able to act as a guide among the channels. If the student is not helped to identify and respond to the qualities of television while in school, it is unlikely that anything in later life will have much influence on his doing so.

A teacher can pick up a strand of a television program and use it in innumerable ways. For example, Dr. Hibbs' closing line about Lorenzo de Medici was that Florence was not free under him, but ". . . it would be difficult to find a better or more pleasing tyrant." Although this comment was doubtless playful, like Mona Lisa's smile, it stemmed from an adult framework that is not accessible to the child. It could leave the child with an erroneous judgment both of Lorenzo's tyranny and of democracy. A skillful teacher can use material of this kind in different classroom contexts.

Teachers can use their students' home television viewing not

---

[13] Charles Winick, "Teenagers, Satire, and *Mad*," *Merrill Palmer Quarterly*, 8 (1962), 183-203.

only as a springboard for discussion of such specifics, but also to provide a framework for responding to the aesthetics of the medium. One framework that we have found useful lies in the three dimensions of form, movement, and content. Form includes the program's internal structure, flow, and cohesiveness. Movement is both visual and auditory. Content is the kind of concern with theme, plot, character, and setting that is traditional in the study of other media.

The school has a responsibility to society and the child in the extension and development of what the child experiences on his screen. A child who depends entirely on television imagery may be less able to develop his own resources for imagery. The school can take an active part in placing television within the larger context of twentieth century life by building on the televiewing that is so important a part of the child's life. Television facilitates the child's entrance into the world of the adult, but the discerning eye of the teacher can point up where the medium's representation of adult life is reasonable and appropriate and where it may be spurious or trivial or brutalized. The teacher, after all, does control the "prime time" of the life of the student.

George Bluestone

Life, Death, and "Nature" in Children's TV

Children's programs conveniently divide, like the adult world they imitate, into vehicles for education and packages of entertainment. Although both operate within narrow, pragmatically defined limits and employ the same tone—mildly amusing, coolly informative, safely clever—information programs tend to cut closer to the bone. Sanctioned by their practical function, they seem less threatening to parents, which leaves the producer freer to explore. Since the general level of children's programing is as low as that of adults, a show with taste, imagination, and honesty seems like a minor miracle. "The Day Life Begins" in ABC's *Discovery* series has been justly praised. Because it stands out from the surrounding landscape, I begin with it as an example of what television can do with freedom, resources, and hard thinking.

Choosing the subject of procreation, the producers made two initial decisions: not to deal directly with animal or human intercourse and to handle everything else without embarrassment. Following these choices, the program moves smoothly from a discussion of one-celled genesis to human birth, tracing a coherent development, making excellent use of film clips and illustrations, combining the intimate format of live TV with the more structured montage of edited film.

The credits, over drawings of buds, bees, and benevolent sun, establish theme and tone. Then Frank Buxton and Virginia Gibson, two clean, healthy, scrubbed Americans whose en-

thusiasm and sincerity are beyond reproach, appear and begin
an informal commentary speaking directly to their listening
audience. Buxton pets a lovable long-eared dog named Cor-
puscle, which becomes an occasion for the text, "Each living
thing gives birth to the same living thing." In quick succession
we see alternate shots of Buxton and Miss Gibson holding, pet-
ting, or observing a cat, lion cub, donkey, fawn, goat, rabbit,
guinea pig, fish, duck, and honey bee. Rapid cutting shows a
wide variety of species as well as the close tactile relationship
between host and pet. What the child will remember is the
harmless innocence of young animals.

Having set up his biological axiom, Buxton goes on to explain that the basic principle of procreation is the division of
cells. We see a paramecium swimming around, then an amoeba
dividing (a fine use of microscopic photography). By showing
how one-celled life reproduces itself, Buxton is able to fix the
choral line, "Life from life."

The host then explains that more complicated forms of life
come not from one organism alone but from eggs. Holding up
a familiar chicken egg, Buxton makes the connection between
the egg and a child, a connection he will return to in the final
third of the program.

Now through the example of turtles he goes on to elucidate
the principle that males and females are required to make life
grow; the father gives something of himself, a sperm cell, and
the mother something of herself, an egg. We cut away to some
excellent footage of the female sea turtle swimming toward
land to lay her eggs. We follow the determined push across
hard terrain, the digging of the nest, the depositing of eggs (120
in number, 1¼-inches across), and finally the return to the
sea. While Buxton explains that many animals are born without their mothers around to help them, we are watching baby
turtles breaking out of their eggs and crawling clumsily into
life.

Another variation is shown through clips of sea horses being
born. This time there is a twist: the mother sea horse deposits
her eggs in the male's pouch, and it is the father who hatches

the offspring. Again a fact is reinforced by striking images: tiny, almost transparent sea horses blowing out of the male's pouch. Such shots move beyond Buxton's quiet narration into the beautiful and marvelous. The impact is highly dramatic, transcending the illustrated lecture to become a felt experience.

At this point, Buxton shows the difference between viviparous and oviparous birth. We see shots of species like the chicken snake, which, as the turtle does, deposits its eggs and abandons them. The host explains that other types, like the diamondback rattler, hatch their offspring in the mother's stomach. Now we witness the first viviparous birth, tiny snakes emerging from the ovum. This step-by-step progression has made the shift both natural and dramatic.

The audience is now prepared for a unique sequence showing a cocker spaniel giving birth to puppies. For television, animal birth is still an unusual subject. To understand how far we have come, we need only recall that a few years ago the birth of a buffalo in Walt Disney's *The Vanishing Prairie* became the occasion for a heated censorship case in New York State. Buxton's scene is cushioned with nursery music, of course, and the womb is continually referred to as "a special place," but what strikes us about the footage on "The Day Life Begins" is its absolute naturalness. It is illuminating to see the spaniel cleaning its puppies, giving them milk from her body, and to be told that the mother has special muscles which help the baby out along the birth canal. The host then informs us that the mother will take care of her baby until it is old enough and strong enough to take care of itself.

We are now ready for the difficult handling of birth in humans. Immediately Buxton points out that human beings are "special," because whereas animals give birth by instinct, the human baby is born "out of love, understanding, and reason." Because humans are a special case, Buxton goes to visit Dr. Milton Levine to ask about the facts of life. Where Buxton is avuncular, Dr. Levine is paternal. The interview takes place in appropriately informal surroundings—green lawns, foliage, summer day. The doctor projects an image of sympathetic wisdom.

At this point Buxton necessarily turns himself into a child, asking the questions of a six-year-old. This shift strains the scene somewhat, but it at least makes credible Dr. Levine's equally childlike explanations. We are now treated to a reprise of principles that have been established in earlier portions of the program. Dr. Levine explains about egg cells and sperm cells, about babies growing in "a special place" below the mother's stomach, about feeding and growth. To show the size of a human egg, the doctor takes out a pencil and punches a tiny hole in a leaf. As he talks about growth, we are shown drawn illustrations of the baby as it looks at three months and at six months. Does the mother experience any discomfort? Frank asks. Some, says the doctor, but because she feels love and because most mothers want their babies very much, the positive feelings far outweigh the discomfort.

Finally we see close-ups of live babies, while the hosts wrap things up: "You were born because your parents love each other and wanted something of themselves to show for their love. When you grow up you will learn to take care of yourself, but you will still feel part of your family." Then their business done, the hosts abruptly say good-bye.

Granting the excellence of "The Day Life Begins," we may have one of two reactions: (1) within television's allowable limits, Jules Power has rendered distinguished service by treating a difficult subject; (2) the program is evasive because it skirts the delicate question of intercourse. The first reaction is clearly justified because in this case we can be grateful for large as well as small favors. "The Day Life Begins" is so effective by comparison that on any relative scale it rates very high indeed. But the second reaction raises a more general question: What attitudes are fostered by most nature films for children?

Certainly Walt Disney, with his flawless eye for the balance between innovation and entertainment, has in his *True Life Adventures* given us our most popular and influential nature films. In the aggregate, films like *Seal Island, Operation Undersea, Jungle Cat, The African Lion, The Living Desert,* and *The Vanishing Prairie,* through theaters as well as television, have set the audiovisual style and tone for nature films.

On the one hand, Disney's superb and dedicated naturalist-photographers have closed in on a world that has never before been seen.

These anonymous heroes who spend months and years shooting in the field have rightly become legends in the trade. Over the years, exercising the patience of Job, they have learned to adapt all the resources of the camera—telescopic lenses, stop-motion action, portable tape recorders—to capturing natural cycles in ways that were inconceivable before the age of motion pictures. For scientists these records have proved invaluable, and for children they offer fascinating information. Paradoxically, the more the child learns about nature the further his sentient experience becomes removed from nature.

Once the raw footage has passed through the able hands of Disney's editors, a transformation takes place. Disney's studio creates a world, an experience that is very different from what any farm boy knows about "real" nature. By shaping the naturalist's raw footage through continuity, music, and narration, Disney creates "entertainments" which place a carefully screened intermediary between spectator and subject. What we get is an elaborate act of personification, a series of fables rather than factual "truth," something much closer to the world of Disney's cartoon characters than to "real" nature. In *The Vanishing Prairie* the narrator *says,* "Nature labels no creature good or bad—she treats all alike." But the film *shows* something else. Mood music, the narrator himself, the contrived patter and continuity built up through editing constantly take sides and clue our reactions.

For example, in the marvelous sequence of the prairie dogs, their tunneled villages are threatened with a variety of predators—owls, rattlesnakes, ferrets, coyotes, badgers, and prairie falcons. The prairie dogs are depicted as sharp, alert, quick, brave, cute, and cunning. In every case the prairie dog outwits, outmaneuvers, or outfights his nemesis. Our sympathy is so clearly on the side of the prairie dog that it would be too up- setting, too cruel to show one of his species getting caught and killed. Through constant selection, favorites in *True Life Ad- ventures* assume the status of characters in fables, like Donald Duck, who for the sake of sympathetic audiences achieve eter- nal life by triumphing over all adversity.

Still, Disney's films inevitably have moments of great power and ambiguity. The cheetah in *The African Lion*, for instance, picks out his prey in a herd of gazelles, takes off like the wind at sixty miles an hour, bypasses luckier victims, and finally, in a swift display of irresistible power, brings down his game. The kill and feeding are kept discreetly at a distance, so that even though the hunt is terrible in its way we are left emotionally free to admire the cheetah's grace. A *beautiful* killer, we feel.

Another example is the mountain lion in *The Vanishing Prairie*. The narrator makes it very clear that the mother hunts only to feed herself and her two cubs, giving us an emotional cushion for the scene where she tracks down and kills a deer. Later, on the prowl again, she approaches an enclosure where a spotted fawn has been left unguarded. By instinct, the fawn lies absolutely still, partially protected by its camouflage. The cougar pauses, smelling, listening, bringing the audience to the edges of their seats, gasping, "No, she wouldn't—she couldn't—." Finally, thinking she has imagined something, the mother lion moves on. The agonizing moment passes. Luck, fate, and accident have conspired to preserve our good opinion of the cat.

For the most part, the endless analogies and allusions to hu- man models create a cutely personalized world. Mountain goats clang horns to the tune of "The Anvil Chorus," otters skitter like children on icy snow, scorpions do a hoe-down, prairie grouse perform a strange Indian war dance, Wagnerian birds a slow-motion ballet. These entertainer's impositions on the natural world lead inevitably to distortion. There is something coy about American nature films that place carefully filtered windows between the child and his "information." Historically, speaking, it is a great step forward to see the birth of buffaloes and cocker spaniels. But not until we devise a way to present realities of neutral savagery and of human intercourse—so far confined to a few well-written books in doctors' offices—will we be able to flatter ourselves that we are educating our children to the facts of life.

That the Disney approach is not the only possible one becomes obvious when we consider films like *Farrebique*, Arne Sucksdorff's *Shadows on the Snow*, and most of Robert Flaherty. All of these do a better job of *rendering* the narrator's line in *The Vanishing Prairie* about nature labeling no creature good or bad. I recognize that what lies behind the difference in shape and tone is ultimately a difference in vision. The argument over whether animals (human or otherwise) need more civilizing or humans more naturalness is not going to be settled by fiat or persuasion. I would merely emphasize, on the basis of the sampling I have seen, that our adult suspicion of the sentient, natural man does pour over into the world we fabricate for children. Personally I am still on Huck Finn's side. We need more lighting out for the Territory Ahead to save us from all the programatic Aunt Sallys who want to "sivilize us."

The "fable" of Disney's prairie dogs leads us to a consideration of animated cartoons which drop all pretense to "informing" and make direct bids for the entertainment market. Here we discover that children's cartoons are an endless repetition of filed movements derived from tested formulas going back to Disney's earliest creations, to Warner Brothers' *Bugs Bunny*, to Chuck Jones' *Tom and Jerry*. Within their limits, these absolutely predictable works, like the zoo and the circus, seem to endure through the years with a regenerative formal charm. Like the root-tale of the gunfight, which seems to hold up under endless permutations and combinations, the formulas of commercial cartoons are so rigidly controlled that true originality becomes as rare as an announcer's *faux pas*. Just as audiences never seem to tire of the Manichean confrontation between western hero and bad man, young children seen impervious to large doses of chase, violence, and escape. All major children's cartoons—*Rocky and His Friends, Bullwinkle, Yogi Bear, Felix, Woody Woodpecker* (*The Flintstones* is a special case I shall discuss later)—work endless variations on a few reliable chords. Rocky perpetually flees Boris and Natasha; Yogi Bear the invaders of Jellystone Park; and Breezely Bruin has endless encounters with the personnel of an arctic military base.

The result is that just as dramatic series are conditioned more by budgets, formulas, and time contingencies than by directors, the styles of animated cartoons seem interchangeable. Movements tend to be lateral and vertical because these are easier to see on a plane surface. There is little use of depth, and perspective is both occasional and obvious. Thus story and style tend to flatten out into two dimensions.

The credits which close *Rocky and His Friends*, with their echoes of Steinberg drawings, are much more imaginative. Like Hitchcock in the thirties, the animator seems to be saying: this is what we could do if only our audiences (agencies?) let us. It is a curious fact of TV viewing that the more utilitarian the image the freer craftsmen seem to be. The real experimentation in the medium goes on in TV's commercials and credits, not in the program proper. The credits in Hanna-Barbera's *Rocky* are analogous to the credits that used to introduce *East Side/West Side*. Visually it is more interesting to watch some of the better auto and hair lotion ads that use zoom shots, rapid dissolves, calculated silences, erotic glances than the images they frame. These merely reflect the same tendency in films (Saul Bass becoming a kind of occult hero for those who *know*) and in the Hanna-Barbera asides.

I am not at all surprised that there is now an exclusive film festival for advertising films. Credits and commercials are "necessary," as *Discovery* is "educational," so no one can accuse the craftsmen of being arty. I have noticed that my friends increasingly watch the commercials, reacting like fans with disgust to those they consider bad and appreciating those that are done with style. It is not at all unusual to find even casual viewers picking out favorite spots, a phenomenon that would have seemed strange ten years ago. Some of the best cutting I have seen appears in those sports sequences that introduce the locker scenes in Vitalis commercials; some of the wittiest use of sound appears in Northwestern Mutual Security ads.

The rigid formulas of animated chase might not alone account for the impoverishment of children's programing if the filed drawings did not, in addition, have to operate within a rigid format. The standard program is usually divided into three four-minute sketches separated by one-minute spot commercials. The assumption seems to be that children in the 4-8 group have short attention spans and are therefore incapable of absorbing more than short bursts of action. Pedagogically this assumption may be right, but the gross effect is to create a world of speed, violence, and absolute predictability at the expense of surprise, charm, and novelty.

The Coyote and the Roadrunner series, showing up in adult art houses, has demonstrated that an extraordinary wit *can* work within the limits of predictability. *Roadrunner* goes *Tom and Jerry* one better by multiplying the absurdity of the Coyote's traps to monstrous, even atomic, proportions. In a world where time, space, accident—and therefore God—are always going for the Roadrunner, attention shifts to the manner, not the matter, of winning. What makes *Roadrunner* attractive to adult audiences are wry asides, precision of timing, freer use of technique—receding landscapes, depth effects, verbal ellipses. The latest Rube Goldberg backfires with as much ingenuity as it was built, leaving the Coyote in midair sheepishly holding up a sign reading "oops." Here the animator both makes his audience an accomplice in artful parody and asks to be admired for his cool professionalism.

We do not know what long-range effects a diet of formula cartoons can have on children. Most surveys have centered on violent dramatic shows because *The Untouchables* worries parents more than *Huckleberry Hound*. Research by Joseph Clapper, Robert Zajonc, Raymond Forer, and others on the effects of television viewing suggests that prolonged exposure is *not* the primary determinant of attitudes and behavior; it is merely an index of attitudes formed by parents, church, school, and neighborhood. Still, it is interesting to look into some of the assumptions of these cartoons. One of my first observations is that the mythology of animation works out as inexorably as a preordained chess game. The heroes of animation are borrowed from a curious mixture of western folklore, historical legend, fairy tales and what, for lack of a better phrase, I will call the mythology of entertainment.

Mr. Peabody and Sherman, in *Rocky and His Friends*, will go back in their time machine to the French Revolution or to the days of Daniel Boone. Peter Potamus, the Hanna-Barbera creation, will restage a satirical version of "Jack and the Beanstalk." Cartoons do not create myths of their own, as Disney's perhaps did by virtue of being first in the field; they are parodistic exploitations of past creations.

When Peter Potamus was announced for the 1964 season, I made the mistake of thinking, like many TV reviewers, that "new" in the mass media could still mean "novel." But when the first program appeared, introducing the typical comic hero of silent films, a clumsy affable character who blunders successfully through all adversity, the sameness of pacing, situation, and style was extraordinary. The new program could take its place, with hardly a change of beat, beside hundreds of others cut from the same cloth. There were the same black-on-gray drawings, the same priority on speed, the same punning, the same format. Peter and So-So, Breezely Bruin and Sneezely Seal; the dogs Yippy, Yappy, and Yahooey, modeled on the Three Stooges—all floated up from the animation boards as easily recognizable as those commercial *entr'actes* which push Ideal Dolls and Corn Flakes. Peter became more unruffled padding for salesmanship, still the real function of television.

The mythology of entertainment assumes a similar place in children's cartoons. Bullwinkle sounds like Red Skelton; Mr. Big, the villain in the Rocky episodes, like Peter Lorre; Peter Potamus like Joe E. Brown. Occasionally there is even a guest appearance, as in an episode called "Duck Seasoning" on the Yogi Bear show, in which an alligator with the voice of Alfred

Hitchcock unsuccessfully pursues a Tweety-type duck. The mythology of entertainment is so assertive, I suspect, because *all* stories, historical legends and fairy tales alike, are filtered through the Great Equalizer known as mass media. Because television is omnivorous for material, it ends by devouring its own offspring.

These allusions to adult personalities (Yogi Bear himself is a pun on the irrepressible former manager of the New York Yankees) is a strange phenomenon considering that with few exceptions they have no function except to wink at parents. They are in-group jokes which reflect, it seems to me, the general condescension we see in so many adult gestures toward children. The animator-huckster seems to be saying: "We adults know what is going on, we know the score. We know the same people, we like the same things, so you can safely trust us with your kids. After all, anyone who loves Red Skelton, Peter Lorre, and Alfred Hitchcock can't be all bad."

Only sustained watching of these programs can suggest how widespread this reaching across the child to the parent can become. The technique helps explain why those programs which constantly win the highest praise of adults, the Hanna-Barbera creations, are famous for their punning. "This Goon for Hire," "Rebel Without a Pause" are titles of episodes on *Rocky and His Friends*, allusive puns that must be incomprehensible to millions of young watchers who have no memory of the original movies.

Another program will retell one of Aesop's fables, the story of the fox and the minks. Three minks devise a technique for evading a wily fox. Whenever the fox appears, the minks climb up on each other's shoulders and hoist themselves into trees just in the nick of time. Gradually the low man becomes weaker and weaker until finally the ladder falls, and the fox exits carrying his quarry. Only at the end do we realize that we have been set up for a weak pun: "A chain is only as strong as its weakest mink."

At first these puns seem really witty, fast, professional, exuberant, but with repeated watching they become sardonic and even menacing. Eventually we encounter the big question about the real function of parody aimed essentially at parents. What lies behind the self-lacerating and almost nihilistic tone?

Parody becomes a dominant mode when the artist finds inherited forms absurd but is prevented from imagining alternatives. Another way of putting it is to say that parody appears when the artist rejects the sanctity of his past but cannot envision a future. Paralleling the vogue of Allen Sherman, who ridicules popular songs by burlesquing their lyrics, TV animators find little sacred within allowable limits. For example, when Mr. Peabody and Sherman rescue Louis XVI from the Bastille, the episode follows the convention of popular entertainment which sees revolutionaries as villains, but the royal personage who is rescued when the heroes smuggle in a huge stack of gunpowder disguised as pancakes is as preposterous as the revolutionaries. Mr. Peabody discovers where the king is being kept by unscrambling an anagram on a piano: "Steel" and "Bas" equal Bastille. Later, in answer to one of Sherman's questions, Mr. Peabody says that "guillotine" is really Gil Otinne, another rebel hero. Like many of Ionesco's characters, he is forever coming up with explanations that never explain anything.

To cite another example, Peter Potamus and his sidekick So-So land on a hillock that turns out to be a shaggy hair of the giant in "Jack and the Beanstalk." As the episode develops, we learn that the giant is an affable moron and that Jack is an avaricious pipsqueak who finally gets what he deserves when he steals a goose that *doesn't* lay golden eggs. The values of the old tale have been cleverly inverted, but to what end?

With a Jonathan Swift or a Jules Feiffer, parody can become healthy and biting satire. But any adult who sits through a steady diet of television cartoons will be struck by the charming cynicism, the sardonic and even sadistic seam which is part of the texture in contrast, say, to the more lovable realistic (and photographed) heroes of Beaver, Lassie, and Flipper. It is as though the animator, bored with endless playbacks of fixed situations, begins working in clever inversions, puns, asides which, being over the heads of the kids, become private signals to co-workers or to "hip" parents who happen to wander in between changing diapers and getting supper. The TV animator knows he is a very skillful craftsman who is in the business of leading sheep, so that much of his style, even his hatred, is directed at an audience for whom he ultimately feels contempt. Is it any surprise that Hitchcock is a kind of underground hero?

True satire is directed against pretension, against institutional automatism, as Henri Bergson showed us a long time ago, but the TV animator is critically hobbled because he must confine his thrusts to harmless popular images, straw men who need little debunking. Playful skepticism directed against safe targets blunts the instruments of satire. It develops an oblique, sardonic stance which becomes unmistakable. The first two or three times I watched *Rocky and His Friends* I was amused and flattered because I got the asides, the puns, and most of the allusions, but after awhile the whole thing palled. I did not understand why until those strategies became visible. When these films are played over and over, even the children get bored and head for the sandbox.

Sometimes this compressed imitation of adult formulas leads to programs aimed at both the adult crowd and children in the ten-to-teen-age group. Both *Mr. Magoo* and *The Flintstones* are now scheduled in the early evening hours, but I am not sure whether this acknowledges the child in the man or the man in the child. As far as I can see, *The Flintstones* is a simple replica of adult situation comedy. The only difference is that the caveman format allows some mild jokes dealing with rocks and stones—Pebbles, and Rubbles, Cobblestone Lane. Everything else works off the prototype of *I Love Lucy*—the blundering husband; the comic earthmother whose superior wisdom keeps the household intact; the bumbling neighbors; the genial emasculation which treats all male deviations as boyish pranks. The formulas are repeated right down to the canned laughter.

In an episode called "The Kissing Burglar," for example, Wilma hears that a thief who has been frightening the neighborhood has a unique style—he kisses his female victims and gallantly leaves each a rose. Wilma makes the mistake of telling Fred that she is intrigued by this romantic criminal. Fred decides to test her by posing as the Kissing Thief himself. Wilma gets wise to the masquerade and plays Fred along to teach him a lesson. Naturally the real burglar appears, and through mistaken identity Wilma has her fling after all with an amorous criminal who makes Fred seem inept. Then we discover that the little man is in fact escaping from a harridan, a sort of Wilma pushed to extremes. After a mix-up with the police, the Kissing Thief insists on going to jail to get a rest from his nagging wife, leaving Fred free to return to Wilma. Domestic harmony has once again been ironically restored. The series consists of similar well-made formulas, but since *The Flintstones* makes a direct bid for adult audiences it lacks the parodistic tension of the children's hour.

Just as the parodistic mode in children's animation has not been sufficiently understood, we need to pay more attention to the conditions of TV viewing. Again there are no controlled studies available about the effects on the young of mechanized storytellers. We have heard a good deal about how parents use television sets as cheap babysitters during the frantic hour, but I think we need to know more about what happens when millions of children hear machine-tooled tales from a flickering box. We have abdicated the art of storytelling—like so many other functions that used to be carried on in the family, the clan, the village—to the professionals and to the occasional bartender, barber, or salesman who happens to be good at it. Between the aged storyteller sitting around a fire or pot-bellied stove and the agency animator lies the history of a wide range of differences in gesture, mood, and technique. In the days before we could pick up the latest Golden Book at the supermarket, children would have a small collection of favorite stories, including perhaps *Winnie the Pooh*, *Black Beauty*, *Treasure Island*, and *The Wizard of Oz*. Very often bedtime stories would consist of improvised sketches by parents whose imagination and ingenuity would be tested every night.

The rise of children's books as a major industry allowed children to retain the warmth and closeness of parents during the ritual story hour, but one of the costs of an endless supply of books, however beautifully illustrated, has been the demise of improvisation and spontaneity. Appropriating the storytelling function, the mechanized fable removes the parent entirely. Without quite knowing why, many parents are troubled by the hypnotic effects of the "box." I suspect that their disturbance has more to do with the relationship between mother and child than with the nature of television. Are parents troubled out of some dim awareness that the child is responding more attentively to the appliance than to *them*? Viewed in this context, the set becomes a rival but one that is too convenient to give up.

Because the fable does not originate with the parent, the child tends to share what he gets only with other children. Parents may be able to identify assumed characters when the kids play Rocky, Bullwinkle, Yogi Bear, or Huckleberry Hound, but the rhythms, the references, the cadences will tend to sound remote and esoteric. In this sense the mechanized storyteller, like the private lyrics of Bob Dylan and the Rolling Stones, has a divisive effect on the family. We have no evidence that TV animation *causes* the irrepressible conflict between parent and child, but I do think it reflects the presence of that "rebel league" which operates as a kind of subculture in our society, exerting its influence on fashions, merchandising, and community services. We sense it in the endless complaints on the part of youngsters and parents alike, each claiming that The Other "doesn't understand me." This divisive feeling is not going to be changed by importuning parents to be good or by moralizing, but I do want to suggest that a close look at "harmless" children's programs turns up repercussions in the fabric of family relations.

Another consideration that needs more attention is the role of the host on children's programs. Every major city has a local personality who loosely stitches together short cartoons with various children's participation gimmicks. He may be called J. P. Patches, Stan Boreson, or Captain Puget; he may wear a clown's costume or a uniform; he may be a fugitive from the sports department or from nowhere, but he will gamely try to create the image of a genial uncle, a more or less reliable baby-sitter. With few exceptions (*Captain Kangaroo* nationally and *The Wunda Wunda Show* in Seattle), all masters-of-ceremony have two things in common: an ignorance of children and an insufferable condescension. Whenever children appear on these programs, they seem so frightened, inhibited, and re-pressed that one has the illusion he is watching a grim charade in a retention home, with the host as a sort of joker-jailer put-ting on a performance for the trustees. This state of affairs in-evitably results when children are treated as consumers in-stead of people. Because the host format uses only second-rate productions that cannot find independent programing, the ani-mated cartoon is reduced to the status of an act in a vaudeville revue. In any case the personality of the host seems to rub off on the guileless cartoon character. Bright children get bored, move on to adult programs or away from television entirely.

The formulas of the animated cartoon might not be so strik-ing if we did not have excellent models to compare them to. There is an extraordinary ferment—sophisticated, inventive—now taking place on a global scale.[1] Measured against the work being done in France, England, Czechoslovakia, Yugoslavia, Japan, and by Ernest Pintoff and John Hubley in the United States, most television cartoons seem simpleminded.

At the Vancouver Film Festival in 1963, for example, the grand prize for best short film went to Bŕetislav Pojar's *The Orator*, as well as a special jury prize "for inventiveness and technical excellence" to a group of eight short French entries. Almost every technique known to the graphic arts is being ap-propriated for animated shorts: steel engravings, wash draw-ings, combinations of live figures and drawn backgrounds, col-lage, puppets, stills, pin screens (applied pointillism), cutouts, mobiles. More important, the virtuosity of these films is insep-

---

[1] For two recent accounts, see "Special Feature: Animation," *Film Quarterly*, Spring 1964, pp. 16-40; and David Rider, "New Lines," *Films and Filming*, September 1964, pp. 12-14.

arable from their sharp, pungent comments on modern life. Their characteristic mode is satire, not parody. Two examples from Vancouver will suggest the range and virtuosity of recent animation.

Pojar's *The Orator* is a puppet cartoon which pokes fun at after-dinner speakers. Papier-mâché faces are stylized, brightly colored. The figures' round, bland contours are evolved in a truly original style. As the orator rehearses at home, boring his thoughtlessly supportive wife who nods approvingly from the bathtub, nonsense syllables, representing his speech, are ballooned into the frame. The sound track is composed of Mc-Laren-type electronic distortions. Beautiful calligraphy counterpoints the orator's pompous rhetoric.

When the orator arrives at the meeting, his audience is quickly bored. His calligraphic nonsense syllables are gradually replaced by the clever dreams and fantasies going on in the heads of his listeners. The frenzy of the orator as he tries to capture his polite but passive audience mounts in intensity until his gestures become violent, aggressive. Finally he must confront the brute fact of his failure. As he leaves the podium, spent and puzzled, we feel that an entire life has been exposed. The effect is a long way from Disney and even from Trnka, who is better known for his puppet films. Only on reflection do we realize that Pojar, using only images and calligraphy, has made a profound comment on the abuses of language.

L'Oeuf à La Coque, by Marc Andrieux and Bernard Brevent, was one of the excellent French entries at Vancouver. Here we have a parable that works perfectly within an unusual combination of terror and charm. An invisible eye scans a de Chirico type desert. We see stones and sand beneath whose apparent calm breathes some kind of subterranean life. Strange lights blink through surrealistic holes. Suddenly an egg appears, begins roving like a fugitive across the scene. Something or someone seems to be trying to trap the egg, which resists more and more furiously. In one stunning shot the egg flings itself at the camera and cracks the lens! But it is a losing battle. In the end the egg cannot escape. It falls down one of the trap holes and, after a long descent and one perfectly timed pause, it serenely surrenders to an egg cup.

One could speculate endlessly on the "meaning" of such a parable, but suffice it to say that the film has something to do with nature's furious resistance to taming. Contrast this with Frank Buxton's egg in "The Day Life Begins" and the difference in vision is startling. Like *The Orator*, *L'Oeuf à La Coque* leaves a vivid impression because the artists have freely created a wholly personal vision.

Examples could be multiplied: Dick Williams' *Little Island*, Yoji Kuri's *Clap Vocalism*, Vatroslav Mimica's *Everyday Chronicle*, Carlos Vollardebo's *Verre Textile*, John Hubley's *Moonbird and the Hole*, Pintoff's *The Violinist* and *The Critic*, Alexandre Alexieff's *The Nose*.

The question immediately arises: Can children "take" such films? My experience has been that since children are much less spoiled by conventions, stock responses, and reflexes, they are more open to genuine novelty. *Begone Dull Care* and *Fiddle-De-Dee*, two Norman McLaren classics, have been successfully shown to delighted school children in the primary grades. It may take *some* training to look at a truly original film, but it seems to me that adults are the ones who are frightened of what may, at first viewing, seem unintelligible.

The real trouble is that due to the complications of distribution these films have a difficult time reaching *any* audience, young or old. Most of them have been discovered at Annency and other film festivals, or by word of mouth, but only a few, like the Hubley and Pintoff films, have done a decent business in the art houses. The problem is to get good films and responsive children together. I can easily imagine a television series in which one or two superior shorts, drawn from global reserves, were presented to young viewers, then supplemented with comments from guests, preferably the animators themselves. It would be years before the backlog of good short films would be exhausted. I would like to see what happens when children are allowed to discuss their feelings in comfortable surroundings under the supervision of trained moderators.

Another possibility for a more creative use of animation is an almost virgin field in the United States: films made by children themselves. Once considered an impossible enterprise in school programs, the continued appearance of low-cost 8 mm and 16 mm equipment has made it possible to bring the materials of film making within reach of modest educational budgets. The pioneering work carried on by Tony Hodgkinson, Don Waters, and Stan Reed in England, under the auspices of the Society for Education in Film and Television, has accumulated a background of practical experience which Americans are just beginning to use. Since 1949, Hodgkinson and his co-workers have been proving that films made by students not only have as much originality, charm, and persuasion as children's painting and theatricals; they also train keen and perceptive audiences. There are now 300 film making programs in British schools.[2] Students who participate in the tough process of making films are bound to develop more demanding standards for the films they see on television and in theaters. So far, film making on the primary school level in the United States is almost nonexistent. Hodgkinson's SEFT has about eight hundred members scattered all over the world, but American membership stands at a mere dozen.[3]

For this reason, the kind of work that Yvonne Andersen has been doing with children in Boston and Provincetown schools appears downright revolutionary. One of the films, made by youngsters in the 7-12 age group and supervised by Mrs. Andersen, is called *The Amazing Colossal Monster*. Characters were made from a jangled combination of paper boxes, pipe cleaners, papier-mâché. Children were taught the right ratios for simulating movement (a painstaking and exacting discipline as any professional knows). They used painted backdrops instead of more cumbersome three-dimensional sets. They used

---

[2] See Tony Hodgkinson, "Children's Films and Screen Education," *Film Comment*, II, 2, 14–18.

[3] For information on SEFT write Professor Tony Hodgkinson, School of Public Communication, Boston University, Boston, Mass. Two useful booklets: *A Handbook for Screen Education* published by SEFT and *Screen Education* (UNESCO, Place de Fontenay, Paris 7e, France).

stylized dialogue, making free and clever use of distortions. Even though coherent sentences are still present, they intuitively arrived at Pojar's technique in *The Orator*. Mrs. Andersen's influence may have been strong in shaping and organizing the film, but essentially the film was written, shot, and edited by the children in a Saturday class.

They invented a parable which is both incisive and refreshing. A strange green monster steps out of a space capsule at an amusement park on earth. His movements and gestures are harmless, but the crowds panic, reacting with fear and horror. Scientists and soldiers combine brains and brawn to track down and destroy the monster, and for a moment it looks as though the tale is going to end with the trite denouement of a thousand science-fiction films. At this point the parable takes a *Dr. Strangelove* twist. The scene shifts to the monster's home planet where a troubled astronomist peers through a telescope. To his chagrin he witnesses the sad fate of the itinerant monster on earth. Indignant, the green-headed scientist orders a retaliatory strike. The last images show startled earthlings staring skyward at an entire squadron of invading space ships obviously intent on wiping us out. Moral: Don't be cruel to monsters who haven't done anything. The mood is not very different from the ending of John Hubley's *The Hole*.

I suspect that making one film is worth a thousand illustrated lectures or predictable entertainments. Parents often have the illusion that superior children's programs are a triumph of progressive education because the subject matter deals with the practical world around us. We forget that John Dewey put a high premium on the sensuous, tactile appropriation of the natural world. Watching the birth of puppies on "The Day Life Begins" will never substitute for the experience of seeing one's own spaniel giving birth. Making a film is a kind of imaginative exercise which involves the child in a range of experiences that passive viewing never touches. Unless a television program, like all great art, returns the child to the substance of his active life, it will never really last. The real drama of children's programs takes place after the set is turned off.

A Twenty-one Inch
Medium for Thirty-six
Inch Receivers

A certain four-year-old of my acquaintance refuses to wear a hat. Rains may blow and winter snows accumulate, but Greg faces them all bareheaded and defiant. He refuses to wear any of the practical headpieces his anxious parents have provided or any of the fanciful hats he has demanded of them. These— pith helmet, space dome, ten-gallon hat, and GI liner—are reserved for watching television. He comes to the set bareheaded but attentive, turns it on and waits. As soon as the raster settles into pictures of cowboys, space men, pirates, or clowns, he rushes to his hat tree and selects the appropriate uniform. He also scoops up a brace of six-shooters, an intercom, or a cutlass. These, too, are reserved for the times when he is given access to the television set.

Peter is eight. He is much too urbane a viewer to be caught dead in a ten-gallon hat. When asked what television programs he likes, he wants to know what *kind* of program the interviewer is interested in. "Something to watch that you *like* or a teaching program?" He says he prefers entertainment programs. He finds *Captain Kangaroo* "amusing. He's funny but he's not funny, funny, funny, makes you laugh like hell (sic)." Peter's favorite program, at the moment, is "part entertainment and I don't know what you'd call the other part. You get ideas."

Peter and Greg are each giving us, in their own ways, the most important instruction which we as teachers or producers need concerning children's programing. Each confronts television as children have always confronted reality, in a context of play. Four-year-old Greg would not be in the least surprised if the cowboys, soldiers, or space men stepped from the set into the living room, or if he were somehow to step into the space capsule. In either event he is ready. He has what he conceives to be necessary to participate. Peter at eight accepts the reality of the tube face insulating him from the world he sees within the box, but he, too, wants to play. His play is internalized. He wants to be entertained. And each wants to apply what he sees to what he believes the world around him to be.

There would seem to be nothing recondite in this observation. Yet what do we see when we examine what most stations pass off as programing for children? Entertainment, to be sure, but not entertainment which gives the child much to work with. When the cartoon comes to its inevitable closing iris, it is followed by a cowboy-clown-cowgirl-pirate-costumed announcer who intersperses commercials with homilies on tooth-brushing or traffic safety. The cowboy-salesman and his employer are alike smugly satisfied that they have served the public interest. They may even have a certificate from the local Dental Society or Safety Council to prove it. This is not to suggest that the station operator feels that he has discharged his obligation to operate in the public interest. No indeed. He contacts those who should be most concerned with child development in his community, who urge that something *elevating* be put on instead of entertainment. The results are often ("Once upon a time Ludwig Beethoven was a little boy . . .") such that no self-respecting viewer, child or adult, would voluntarily watch. The station collects another certificate, and the children go back to watching cartoons. Who can blame the station manager, in the face of such experience, for sadly being reinforced in his belief that cartoons are all his audience really wants?

Unfortunately, neither the station manager nor the forces in the community apt to be most critical of him have stated the problem correctly. For the problem is not really providing an alternative to entertainment. For one thing, the children simply won't accept it. If there is another channel available to them, they will turn to it. Furthermore, there is nothing, our Puritanical heritage to the contrary notwithstanding, intrinsically wrong with entertainment. The problem, properly stated, is how entertaining programs can be designed to make use of television's unique abilities to provide children with insights into the nature of the world about them.

An early and generally a very successful attempt to do just that was the ambitious CBS network series *Let's Take a Trip* with Sonny Fox. This series rested on no a priori considerations as to what was already within a child's frame of reference but rather sought to broaden that frame. For thirty minutes each week children throughout the country were able to go to places and learn about things which they would normally have no opportunity to do. *Let's Take a Trip* took a trip each Sunday afternoon; one week to the Indonesian Embassy, another week to Jacques Lipchitz' studio, another week to the foundry where a piece of his sculpture was being cast. Foreshadowing, as it did, the mobility of television which film cameras, satellites, and video tape have now permitted us to take for granted, the program represented a monumental achievement for its time.

It would be gratuitous, years after the fact, to cavil with such an ambitious series. *Let's Take a Trip* has long since left the air and is hardly in a position to defend itself against any criticisms. Furthermore, our vantage point makes it too easy to overlook the enormous problems involved in doing a live electronic remote at a different location each week, oftentimes in a different city. If kinescope recordings of the program look cold today, if they seem remote or sometimes lacking in poise, these faults can surely be ascribed to the paleotechnic era in which they were produced. In television eight or ten years is a long, long time. There was no such thing as video tape recording when *Let's Take a Trip* just came on the air. The program had to be produced at the time it was to be shown; what happened during that thirty minutes appeared on the home screens, jumbles, mistakes, delays, and all. Nowadays, the program would undoubtedly be videotaped. Pacing would (hopefully) be determined by dramatic necessity and not by such considerations as having to allow time to wheel a hundred pound camera into the next room, set the wheels of its dolly, and refocus it. Most especially important for our concern, the program's host would be free to concentrate on the material. He would not be distracted from guests or content by such concerns as whether that camera was on time moving into the next room, and if it weren't what would he say to fill the time?

Sonny Fox's distraction could be dismissed as an awkwardness of production, of understandable if regrettable origin, but a mere mechanical detail in an ambitious program of long ago. But what shows up as failings in the kinescopes, if viewed in terms of our concern with how television can be used to hold children's attention, may prove particularly instructive in thinking about today's and tomorrow's programs. For if Sonny Fox's concern with something unseen off camera is distracting to the adult viewer, what can it have been to the child? Surely it must have communicated itself to some degree and its message must have been unmistakable: there is something to which you are not privy which is much more important, more engrossing than what you are seeing. Similarly, the extent to which Pud and Ginger, the two children who joined Sonny Fox in his trips, were used as props rather than as real children, the extent to which they became victimized by the mechanics of the situation, seriously affected the program's credibility and entertainment for the audience. If they had any function at all it was a surrogate audience, and if your representative does not seem interested, how can you be persuaded that there is something worthy of your attention?

The question which those two youngsters should pose for us is one of how we are to regard the children in our audience we wish to reach. Are we to expect them to take their cues from adults, or are we to be sensitive to them? Granted, adults know more about what children need, but surely no parent can honestly admit that he or she always knows when the child will accept help in meeting the need. The youngsters on *Let's Take a Trip*, when they are apathetic or disinterested, show us clearly what they have failed to respond to. In the final analysis, since we are considering recreational time when children and not adults are apt to be in control of the receiver, we cannot allow the good intentions or the ambitiousness of concept, or the intrinsic interest to the adult of the subject matter, to blind us to the fact that ultimately the child viewer must be entertained enough to watch.

In 1964 the most popular children's program in Philadelphia was a series on mental health entitled *Tottle*. Produced in cooperation with the local mental health association and employing a consulting psychologist, it was chosen in preference to cartoon programs on two other channels by more than 70 percent of the children then available to watch. Although it appeared at 9:30 Sunday mornings, its rating was as high as any locally produced program in the area. It attracted full commercial sponsorship and was regularly viewed by nearly 800,000 children from five to ten.

Now surely this is an aim which anyone concerned with child development could applaud, and a performance record which any commercial broadcaster would envy. But it could never have come about without the abandonment of several cherished preconceptions. The project demanded the setting aside of immediate mass acceptance as a criterion of success. Furthermore, it required the abandonment of notions as to what constituted formal teaching on television. Obviously, teaching children how to handle their feelings could not be equated with teaching them how to handle their pencils.

The problems with which the program sought to deal (sibling rivalry, coping with fears, accepting individual differences, testing one's worth) bothered children long before there were television systems to attempt to assuage them, and for centuries children have resorted to the same kind of raw material to help them work through their anxieties in fantasy. The literature on the function of mythology and the studies on cross-cultural themes in fairy stories are too extensive and too well known to bear repetition here, but surely they suggest that there exists a viable tradition to serve as a model for the producer. If the fairy story, still sufficiently removed to be nonthreatening, could be made to relate directly to twentieth century American children, predominately urban, cut off from the security of a sense of *Gemeinschafft* which even their parents enjoyed, subjected to the pressures of an ever more competitive, conformist, consumer-oriented society, it might not be teaching in a fashion which television was accustomed to, but teaching it would be—teaching which made use of the very best opportunities the medium presents.

Once the appropriateness of fantasy has been accepted, the rest of the production details are readily inferred. What better way to handle fantasy for children on television than with puppets? They don't present the prohibitive cost problems of animation; they are more easily obtained, directed, and shaped to the ends of the producer than live actors; they are three-dimensional and scaled to the television screen. Twenty-three such puppets, forest creatures rather than completely literal animals, make up the cast of *Tottle* and move through a meticulously consistent world not too dissimilar to that of the human five-to ten-year-old viewer. The basic characters are a brother and sister and their parents, their schoolmates, teacher, and other adults with whom they are apt to come into contact. Each program deals with a particular problem as it affects several of the characters. Although the adult puppets may sometimes function as wiser and more experienced creatures, no one points out a moral, no one preaches or lectures. The point is there and invariably shown in more than one context for them to understand and accept if they will. What distinguishes the program from those designed solely to entertain is that every story is first subjected to a searching analysis, not on the basis of whether the young viewers will enjoy it, but as to whether it shows them something about the situations—coping with a bully, accepting religious differences, developing good work habits, experiencing the death of a pet, cheating—which they may meet in their own lives. After that analysis, the program is considered in terms of whether or not it pays—whether or not the dramatic outworking in which characters fail because of poor attitudes and decisions or succeed because of healthy ones—is interesting enough to hold the children's attention.

It is difficult to measure the effect of a program like *Tottle*. It does not produce quantifiable results; it may not even lend itself to direct discussion as a program on space flight hardware might. Following President Kennedy's assassination, a program on the death of a loved one was rerun several weeks in succession. A number of parents chose to write in appreciation contending that the program had helped their children adjust to the national shock. It would be reassuring to accept the statements at face value (after all, the program was rerun with that very end in view), but perhaps these parents are merely reporting that their own sense of guilt at being unable to find ways to deal with the topic of death was somewhat alleviated. Although this, too, would serve a useful purpose, it would not be sufficient to consider that the program had succeeded. *Tottle* is addressed to children, and one of the most enticing traps its production staff has learned to eschew is that of producing a program oriented to the audience's parents. Whatever *Tottle* has accomplished, it has succeeded in entertaining, as its vast audience proves. If the entertainment is based on scrupulously examined content, professionally and sensitively guided, some assistance in meeting the child's problems or in developing a personal set of values is bound to filter through. If you hold, as I do, that television can never present a neutral signal, that at every instant it partakes of and reflects some value system, the opportunity and the responsibility are inescapable.

The fantasy of *Tottle* is successful entertainment not because children respond to fantasy in all contexts, but because they require it in some. Miss Twinkles, standing between the Giant Toothbrush and the Gold-Star-for-Today-Board, could simper from now until signoff admonishing young viewers not to be afraid of the dark, not to pummel baby sisters, or not to worry about mother or father abandoning them, but no child would be engaged by the homily long enough to entertain the slightest thought of following her exhortations, for this is subject matter for which the child characteristically draws upon his own fantasy mechanisms.

My young friend Greg, whose experiences I drew on earlier, can teach us still another valuable lesson. He does not preselect his hat for watching television; rather he determines the subject matter and then chooses the appropriate headgear. So, too, if we are to produce television designed to inform or enrich the audience in this age group, we must learn to particularize our hat.

Effective television for children is created in exactly the same fashion as effective television for adults. Both must proceed from the imperatives of the medium. These two statements would seem to be such obvious truisms as not to bear repetition, were it not that our eyes and ears tell us that much of what is broadcast fails entirely to take into account the nature of television. The most distinguishing characteristic of television is that it is not essentially reportorial but presentational. Television's cameras are directional and must be positioned. Consequently, what television shows is not whatever randomly happens before it, but what it actively seeks out. Because of this, the medium must participate, intentionally or unintentionally, at every point in shaping the content of the program.

Perhaps the clearest example of the effect of an understanding of the presentational nature of the medium was seen in the televising of the 1961 Presidential inauguration. One of the networks started with the assumption that television's task was to report—to let it happen and make no comment. Another network started with the assumption that its task was to present an event, a ceremony, which had a shape and a meaning. Both networks showed the burning podium and Robert Frost's touching struggle against age and the elements, but while one network's program managed to convey a sense of the whole event, distinguishing between moments of solemnity and interludes of relaxation, the other succeeded only in presenting home movies of Mrs. Kennedy's hat. Unillumined by any sense of the presentational nature of the medium, that network made no distinction between prayer, oath, speech, parade, or anthem.

It was this failure which was responsible for the much criticized close-up of Mrs. Kennedy's nose twitching during a solemn moment of prayer.

The second characteristic of television I would call attention to is that it is essentially competitive. By this I don't mean to prate on as an apostle of the obvious and point out that CBS and NBC are fiercely in contention for audiences and advertisers. When I speak of its competitive nature, I refer to the fact that television competes with all else that the audience might possibly do with a given thirty minutes or hour of time. Television differs from film in that the film audience has demonstrated a commitment by its very presence; so, too, does television's competitive nature make it different from radio. Unlike radio, television is basically nondiscursive. The viewer is unable to tolerate tangential matter, unable to turn his attention on and off and allow the program to recapture his interest at its own time. Consequently, television places an inordinate premium on clarity and specificity of structure. The very size of the screen focuses the viewer's attention on every detail and demands that each relate to the whole.

Television for children or adults which is to be something other than chewing gum for the eyes can only be developed from a recognition of this principle. The primary purpose of the program must be articulated unequivocally and every production choice made in relation to it. This is the only way to guarantee that we are wearing the proper hat when we approach a particular project and that appropriate choices are made.

Several years ago, we became intrigued at WCAU-TV in Philadelphia, by experiments in teaching reading to preschoolers. As we accumulated reports on the increased interest in the Montessori method, Omar Khayyam Moore's use of typewriters in New Haven, and Glenn Doman's work with brain-damaged children in Philadelphia, we concluded that if a way were found to enlist television in preparing youngsters for school, we would be performing a much needed service.

On September 16, 1963, we launched a weekly series entitled *Love to Read*, a frankly experimental program. We were not so rash as to believe that television could teach preschoolers to read, but we felt that we probably could provide them with some incentive to try, and we certainly could increase reading readiness.

Any program designed to impart basic reading, number, and vocabulary skills to preschool children in an urban environment could not evade the responsibility of addressing itself to those members of the audience who were most in need of the stimulus, the raising of expectations, and the preventive education experience which the program might be expected to provide. Accordingly, *Love to Read* was designed with a twofold purpose. Not only would it deal with the subject matter indicated, but it would address itself especially to the so-called "culturally deprived."

Given the purpose of the program, the format was very easily determined. What could be more appropriate in a program designed to ready students for school than a teacher working directly with the audience? But this would not be enough to hold the children's attention, or to indicate how they should respond to the teacher in a formal school situation since they had no prior experience of school to serve as a model. There is abundant evidence to suggest, however, that children turn to television for examples of the behavior of the age group they are about to enter. Teenage dance programs such as *Bandstand* have proved to be astonishingly popular with younger children. These programs are in part credited for the development of the new very substantial preteen popular record market. This should not really surprise us if we examine how children in any culture find play materials. The American girl playing house, the Havasupai Indian playing "cup and pin" with a rabbit's skull, or the Veeda boy in Ceylon playing at honey-getting are consciously or unconsciously attempting to develop skills which they think will fit them for later life. They consider their play to be, as Montaigne observed, "the most serious business of childhood" just as do those youngsters who come to the television set expecting to see what older children do.

Naturally enough, we added a studio class of three- and

four-year-olds. In addition to their serving as school children models, they also served as a control group providing feedback and a criterion of pacing for the television teacher. Because of our especial interest in those members of the audience who were most in need of the kind of enrichment which the program might provide, the group was variegated ethnically and racially. The teacher, a most gifted young woman, happened to be a Negro. A heavier-than-usual promotion of the subject matter through the ethnic press and mailings to organizations who expressed some commitment to working in the area of intergroup relations were the only other steps which we deemed advisable for reaching this particular segment of the audience. To judge from the mail, we were apparently successful. Requests for materials offered came in about equal numbers from upper middle class, predominantly white areas and from neighborhoods known to be almost exclusively Negro and Puerto Rican. Since most of the children in the studio class were recruited from families who had youngsters in the Great Cities Improvement Program Schools, the backgrounds they brought to *Love to Read* and the questions they asked could be assumed to be representative. Obviously no other reference to this segment of the intended audience was made on the air.

Love to Read was conceived of as frankly experimental, and we sought help from as many sources as we could find. We drew regularly on the experiences of Glenn Doman and Dr. Carl Delacotta of the Institutes for the Achievement of Human Potential, and we retained Miss Rita Ciotti, Language Arts Consultant for the Ford Foundation GCIPS, as a consultant for the series. We tried and discarded many techniques. One of the first to go was that of having the teacher work with the entire studio class. Involving six children diverted her attention and the home audience's attention from the subject matter. The one-to-one or at most one-to-two relationship proved much more productive. Another technique which was discarded early was interrupting the substantive material with physical activity or unrelated games. The children in the studio, and presumably those at home, were there for the primary content of the program and seemed to resent what they took to be distractions. Keeping the individual activities very short and alternating the children with whom she worked seemed to answer the problem of short attention span on the part of the preschool audience. Since it was felt that only a limited number of new symbols or concepts could be introduced each week, the real challenge was finding a variety of simple but effective ways to present the same material several times during the course of any single program. Some of the particularly successful devices were large cards labeling parts of the body and furniture in the studio, letters or words which could be traced with the finger on the face of the home tube, instructions to find something in the room beginning with a particular letter, a guessing game involving picnic baskets whose contents were objects all beginning with the same letter, and a post office in which one of the studio children would respond to instructions from another to surrender packages appropriately labeled. Every few weeks the words which had been studied were collected and augmented with certain proper nouns to form a short story. Copies were offered to the children at home who would join with the studio class in reading it aloud. More than ten thousand illustrated copies of "Coco the Cat," "Topper the Turtle," and "Holding Hands" have been distributed.

As with *Tottle*, we can measure the number of children who watched *Love to Read*, but we can never accurately measure the effect which the program may have had. *Love to Read* was subsequently sent to other CBS-owned stations in New York, Los Angeles, Chicago, and St. Louis, where it seems to have enjoyed much the same reception as it initially received in Philadelphia. Requests for the books have been numerous, and the mail has been enthusiastic. One of the most interesting letters to come out of the exchange program came from a lady in California who said she was particularly grateful to the program since it provided her suburban child with the only experience he had ever had of encountering a Negro who was not relegated to the role of a servant.

In Philadelphia, though, we had the opportunity to observe

the program somewhat more closely. During the summer we reran the series using still another novel approach to the problem to which it was addressed. Several viewing locations were set up in hard-core, multiproblem areas. They were staffed with teachers from Home & School Councils and from neighborhood groups. The Emergency Aid, a volunteer social service agency, supplied teachers' assistants. The Free Library of Philadelphia provided training sessions and shelves of suitable books. The city's Department of Recreation and various other agencies offered locations, and WCAU-TV provided television sets for any neighborhood which requested them. In one instance where there was no available viewing space, the station rented and equipped a bus to stand at a prominent street corner. Mothers were encouraged to bring their children, watch the program, and receive guidance for follow-up instruction. Another session based on the material introduced in the program was held later in the week. Perhaps because the activity was late in starting, the results were numerically disappointing, but groups of up to fifty did meet regularly at least twice a week throughout the summer, sometimes in unbelievably inclement weather. As a result of the experience, the city of Philadelphia requested that *Love to Read* and its follow-up sessions be made available to its Human Renewal Program. It is not inconceivable that *Love to Read* and the climate which it created played some small role in persuading the Philadelphia Board of Education to request a million and a half dollars to set up prekindergarten schools for the culturally disadvantaged. Inez Gottlieb, *Love to Read's* producer, has been asked to chair the Board's advance planning section of the day care center advisory committee.

The next fall we replaced *Love to Read* with a successor program, *Love to Learn*. This went into basic science concepts. Again we used a teacher, this time a peripatetic one with a young friend, who explored the real world around them. Their Socratic dialogue led them into such areas as probability, chemical bonds, Mendelian principles, ecology, and economics. Once again, the problem is stated in terms of finding *the* appropriate way to translate the idea into effective television. For this series, though, we expected our audience to represent a somewhat broader age range. Consequently, we abandoned the teacher-classroom relationship and established a situation in which a wiser and more experienced man (actually a highly successful science teacher who is currently serving as principal of a Philadelphia public school) and a child jointly engaged in problem solving. To demonstrate simple machines they attempt to roll a heavy oil drum onto a platform by means of a plank. When they are seen to become actually exhausted by this unsuccessful activity, they arrive at using the wedge. To explore theories of money, several children are asked to parlay sheep, chickens, and corn to accumulate as many goods as they can. When they have the physical experience of discovering how awkward barter can be, a gold standard is introduced and they trade the items for gold bricks. When they have accumulated more bricks than they can successfully store, they are permitted to bring them to a safe where the teacher issues paper certificates to prove that he has received them.

To demonstrate the effects of the optical system in the human eye, two programs have been created. In the first, the teacher and his friend arrive at and construct a camera obscura in the classic sixteenth century mold. The series goes on to explain groups, sets, and rings, Newton's second law, and the principles of evolution. *Love to Learn*, like its predecessor, *Love to Read*, was well received. But I think its real significance is that it demonstrates what I should like to set down as an axiom: there is no such thing as an idea which cannot be presented to children on television; it is merely necessary to discover the effective and appropriate way to present it.

Early in my own television career, I found myself writing a thirty-minute weekly children's program, designed as a commercial vehicle and built around an irrepressible clown who was unaware of his own limitations and constantly running headlong into reality. Although we soon had a very popular program which delighted the local dairy sponsoring it, it had almost no support from the station carrying it in terms of budget, facilities, or staff. Correspondingly, it was relatively free from management control, and the producer and I had, or thought we had, almost free reign in the selection of subject matter. About this time the massive Picasso retrospective came to the local museum. I brought in an armful of prints and built a program around our clown's efforts to paint his own Picassos. The script looked good on paper, the actors played it fully, and the 200 children in the studio audience that Saturday morning responded with delight. I had every reason to suppose that I was about to be congratulated when I was summoned to the Program Director's office the following Monday; I was totally unprepared for what ensued. For forty-five minutes I was forced to defend the program, unsuccessfully, against charges of having indulged my own taste at the expense of the audience. Picasso, I was told, was totally beyond the comprehension of the five- to ten-year-old.

Two weeks later, I was again summoned to the Program Director's office. This time he apologized. He had been driving past the museum with his own five-year-old who begged to be taken there. She wanted to see the Picassos, she told him. Questioned as to why, she said she had seen the paintings on the program and she liked them. "Picasso wants to see both sides of the lady at once. Or maybe the top and the bottom of a table." Thoroughly persuaded by his daughter's reaction inside the museum, the Program Director gave us carte blanche, and our clown went on to explore the intricacies of simple mechanics, mathematical models, and archaeology. When his enthusiasm allowed him to be misled by a rusty street flare into thinking that he had found a relic of an ancient civilization, and he proceeded to dig his way into a subway station, it may all have seemed like good, clean fun to our audience, but I strongly suspect that some of them came away from their television sets with a rudimentary insight into historical research.

Fortunately, the climate in commercial broadcasting has changed considerably since those days. Stations throughout the country are experimenting with subject matter of a little more complexity than "Let's meet the firemen." NBC's *Exploring* has tackled such subjects as basic logic and the fundamentals of the Binary numbers system. A survey revealed that on the particular day when the Binary system was explored, using the Ritts Puppets, a machine with five lights which they could turn on and off, and a pile of jelly beans, that portion of the program received the highest degree of audience attention. Increasingly, the broadcaster is coming to realize that the only limitation on the ideas which can be presented to young children is imposed by lack of creativity on the part of those who shape the programs.

Unfortunately, the ambiguous mandate under which the broadcaster operates the program "in the public interest" places a heavy onus on the educator. There are innumerable vocal, well-intentioned members of any community who are anxious to express to the broadcaster what they feel to be the public interest. Regrettably, these people are all too often functionally illiterate when it comes to television, and there must be a countervailing force to persuade the broadcaster that good intentions and "elevating" subject matter are not enough.

Children come to the television set with their hats on; they are ready to be enriched and they expect to enjoy it. If what they encounter under the guise of programing designed to educate or enrich them is not satisfactory, if it is not imaginative and engrossing, if it is not good television, if it does not recognize that television is essentially a presentational medium—then they will turn to programs which are, in the long run, of far less social usefulness.

The real lesson which children teach us about teaching them on television is one which has become as apparent to the best practitioners in television as in any other medium: content can never be completely disassociated from manner of presentation since the two interact at every point in the process.

American popular culture has rightfully been described as the most strident in the world. Television is no exception. It simply will not go away. It will continue to be a major force in shaping our children's attitudes and in providing them with raw material on which they will draw for the rest of their lives. Unless tastes have been developed, children will not select for better content. They may be seeking for programs which cater to their traditional needs to explore the world through play, to participate, to be entertained, but they will select for the more effective presentation.

One of the more frightening findings reported by Gary Steiner is statistical support for the belief that most American parents tend to regard the television set as a convenient baby-sitter. Such findings suggest that parents are perfectly willing to submit to the forces in our society whose interests are not in producing television for enrichment and enjoyment, but for consumption. Someone must bolster the broadcasters' inclination to present a more meaningful product. Who is better fitted than the educator whose training and commitment have prepared him to develop a set of criteria which derive from the nature of the medium and to acknowledge the needs of the young audience? If those needs are not satisfied but merely exploited on their most superficial level, we have to envision a diurnal passivity affecting a whole generation of 36-inch consumers. And some day, that generation will grow to manhood.

Brother Thomas Timothy, F.S.C.

The Story of a Newspaper Man: Diary of a Lesson Planned

The focal point of this whole article is concentrated on the word *taught*. A film was taught. This film based on the life of Thomas W. Braden, editor, publisher, and owner of the Oceanside, California, *Blade-Tribune*, was taught to a senior English class of thirty-two college-bound male students of St. Mary's College High School, Berkeley, California, during Thanksgiving week 1963 while the National Council of Teachers of English annual convention was in session in San Francisco.

I taught this film to my senior English class in order to assist an NCTE preconvention workshop on mass media evaluate the possibilities of teaching films to secondary school students. Again I speak of teaching this film. I think it is important to mention that I had never attempted to teach a film before. At best I was dubious about the whole enterprise. My best doubts became my worst fears when I privately previewed this film upon its arrival from Hollywood. There was nothing to teach. I viewed it again to make sure, but my second viewing only confirmed by first judgment: there was nothing to teach.

What follows in this article then is the substance of what both teacher and student learned about films and their place in a classroom. At a teachers' convention I attended recently, an address was given on the nature of learning. The lecturer insisted that the best of learning happened when both teacher and students shared simultaneously in the discovery of truth. This was the case with my teaching *The Story of a Newspaper Man.*

The Lesson Learned

It must be a pedagogical maxim that the lesson planned is not always the lesson taught, and yet no teacher worthy of the name attempts to teach without a plan. My first impressions of the film *The Story of a Newspaper Man* left me afloat and rudderless. I was committed to carry out the assignment of teaching the film, but I simply did not know where to begin. That was Sunday evening. Monday afternoon I cautiously approached the convention workshop session on mass media with the only available print of the film. I presented my problem, we screened the film, a brief discussion ensued, homework was given and a timetable devised. The workshop teachers were to draw up a lesson plan for their homework that night. At 9:00 a.m. the following morning, Tuesday, the first item on the agenda was an hour's discussion on how to teach the film. I listened most attentively as the minutes passed and my "moment of truth" approached. I was due back at St. Mary's High School in Berkeley at 10:30 a.m. to teach the film to my English class. With best wishes and all the good luck the teachers could muster, they presented me with their lesson plans and sent me speeding back across the San Francisco-Oakland Bay Bridge to Berkeley. The panic was gone now, the fear had fled, the disbelief was supplanted by hope and anticipation. The convention discussion and the teachers' lesson plans were concrete assets for the task at hand.

The Lesson Taught

It is quite difficult to totally and accurately chronicle two hours of class discussion. I only intended to submit those opinions and conclusions which the students adhered to as a group after our class dialogue, which on some points took many minutes of argumentation before a consensus was reached. The only preparation for the day's intellectual labors was my comment: "Today I want to teach you a film." The students were pleased, not because they were going to be taught anything, but rather at the delightful prospect of watching a movie; a pleasant change from the normal classroom routine. They presumed that my use of the word "teach" was a phrase employed merely by habit; and in the context of my sentence they were sure I really did not mean it when I said I would teach the film.

So at 10:30 a.m. the students viewed *The Story of a Newspaper Man*. Their first reaction was quite similar to my own. Some asked if there was really something teachable. Others resented my intent to teach what they had seen for themselves. They thought it highly impertinent of me to try "to dig some important meaning" from the cinematic rendition of Tom Braden's life as a newspaper man. As one bright young lad put it: "Why can't we accept it at face value for a change?"

Indeed, why not? This was the very essence of the problem of the mass media, especially of television. The class was most at ease and quite satisfied to accept the whole film in passive torpidity. They argued that the film was interesting and informative, that this must have been the purpose of the producers, that there was nothing subtly philosophical here, and therefore there was nothing to teach. I could sympathize with them, for I had thought this myself not twenty-four hours before.

The interplay of one student's comments upon another's as I asked for their subjective reactions to the film finally led the discussion to some meaningful topic. While some considered the film informative, others felt it should have been more so. One young man thought it was simply a concise documentary of a man's life, but not much more. This was countered by a remark seemingly out of place: "I can't see what's important about a small town newspaper in English class." Someone was quick to ask a more general question. "Can this example of a small town newspaper be applied to all small town newspapers;

or, more important, do the principles Braden uses in running his newspaper apply to all newspapers and their editors?"

The discussion had begun in earnest. This was an important question, but it stimulated a more basic question in relation to our film: "What was the purpose of the film?" The class had already presented two possibilities: a concise biography of Thomas W. Braden or a brief documentary on newspapers. It took some time to resolve this argument. The class debated for almost twenty minutes trying to decide just where the emphasis in the film lay. Other possibilities arose. Some thought it a persuasive vocational film aimed at generating interest in journalism as a profession. A few judged the emphasis to be on the power of the newspaper in a community. Still some others strongly felt it was certainly a biography of Thomas W. Braden made with the intent of boosting higher into political realms. The advocates of the Braden biography theory argued that the title of the film was in their favor. It was the story of a newspaper. The retort came back that the title should include the name of Thomas Braden if the intent of the producers was to feature the owner of the *Blade-Tribune*. But these young men had a most difficult time explaining the multiple sequences dealing with the Braden family so prominent in the film. These shots put emphasis on the man. Furthermore, it was argued, if the film was meant to be a documentary on newspapers, then why was the Oceanside *Blade-Tribune* the only one mentioned? These students also noted that the film dealt with the actual operation of the printing of a day's copy of the *Blade-Tribune* during the last eight or ten minutes of the film, not enough to conclude emphatically that this was the main objective of the producers.

By this time the boys were quite absorbed in resolving this essential question, the purpose of the film. Gone were the resentments against having to think seriously about a film; and, whether they realized it or not, gone was their passivity. They were being taught; better, they were learning. I only had to keep the dialogue on a logical and meaningful trend so that their important questions might be properly answered.

Finally, another question arose which superseded the above consideration because it put the argument into clearer focus and broader perspective: "Is the man the newspaper?" "Can we say that Thomas Braden is the *Blade-Tribune*?" Most agreed that there was strong evidence in the film to substantiate this position. At the very opening of the film when the narrator is first introduced, he comments that a newspaper "informs, persuades, and entertains. In Oceanside, California, the newspaper is one man: Thomas W. Braden, owner, editor, and publisher." The students noted in favor of this argument that Braden's personality dominated the paper and his staff, that he had the greatest influence on the *Blade-Journal*, that it was he who made the paper a success, that the power of the newspaper was in reality entirely in the hands of this one man, and that his triple title of owner, editor, and publisher strongly supported this concept.

The next question followed very logically. Since the newspaper is so important to and influential in a community, and since we believe that essentially the newspaper (in a small town at least) is the man, then it is terribly necessary to know what kind of man the editor is. "What kind of a man is Thomas W. Braden?" Various incidents, scenes, and dialogue from the film were used by the students to corroborate the characteristics which they attributed to Tom Braden. They considered him to be a man of determination and drive whose choleric personality well suited him for the work he did and the goals he had set for himself. They admired him not only as a man who accepted the responsibilities of his position as editor of a newspaper and father of a family but also as a man who enjoyed these responsibilities. The boys judged him dedicated to his profession. Some thought him a "born politician." According to other students, Tom Braden's most attractive characteristic was his decisiveness. A few commended his leadership ability and his inspirational manner. One student found Tom Braden to be a righteously ambitious man. All conceded he was truly human and hence very believable. (Perhaps the most obvious and flattering characteristic pointed out by the students was the man's integrity.) They considered Tom Braden to be a man of principle whose life was absorbed in a profession to which he had made a personal, meaningful, and lasting commitment. They admired the conviction in Tom Braden as he resolutely refused to sell his newspaper to the broker though it was then worth a million dollars. He would not betray himself by selling the newspaper because running the *Blade-Tribune* is what made him most happy. The students recalled almost all of the dialogue between the broker and Braden in substantiating their judgment. Braden's comment that there is something immoral about buying and selling newspapers crystallized this quality of integrity for the students. They remarked how it so clearly indicated Braden's values: (1) there are things in life more important than money; (2) responsibility to the community must not be superseded by personal gain. One boy stated that the morning's discussion was worth our time and consideration if only for the realization of these two principles. There was some agreement here, but most thought the profit came in focusing their attention to a close analysis of something they habitually took for granted. By now we had discussed for a full hour and were running into the lunch period. Not Thomas Braden, nor a good film, nor a stimulating class dialogue can compete with the bell which signals the noon lunch hour.

The afternoon school schedule at St. Mary's High School is comprised of three forty-five-minute class periods. I had all three of them at my disposal to continue teaching *The Story of a Newspaper Man.* I showed the film to the class again at 12: 30. This time they were instructed to bring pencil and paper to jot down quick notes concerning certain cinematic techniques. The sequence of scenes, the continuity of the film, use of symbols or visual imagery, the time, the tempo and the mood, the acting, the music, the opening and closing, the juxtaposition of scenes, all these they were told to observe. I told them to pay more attention to the use of the camera than anything else: how, where, when, and why was the camera employed. They were asked to detect the relationship between the sounds heard and the scenes viewed in order to see clearly the film maker's methods of transition as well as the film's continuity. These students had been taught that all good art possesses the quality of integrity or wholeness. Each separate part of a play or a poem or a short story must contribute to the purpose and wholeness of the work thereby adding to its beauty, its truth, its completeness. I directed them to employ this same analytical technique to the film since we could consider it a work of creative mind, a work of art. With this introduction they witnessed *The Story of a Newspaper Man* a second time.

It was easy to begin our second hour of discussion. The students tended to shift quickly from topic to topic because they had noted so many techniques of the film and, of course, in the film they do not follow a sequential pattern. I first asked about the opening and closing of the film. Several still shots of Braden are used at the beginning and end as the credits and titles are superimposed over them. The boys noted they were the same stills in both instances and that each of them was "lifted" from the live action of the film. One still showed Braden at work in his office, and the second viewed him standing on the beach with his son. This introduced the concept of continuity, so I asked the students for other examples. The constant reference to time both in Braden's own voice on the soundtrack ("There's never enough time.") and the close-ups of the different clocks while the paper is readied for printing answered my question. Students discovered that portions of the picture followed a chronological sequence so that time was the means used to produce a definite continuity. I had to ask them specifically for the three main divisions of the film which contribute so heavily to its continuity. It took time for the class to come up with the triple division used in the outline of the film in the first part of this article. Once they grasped this, one lad was ready to explain the moral continuity of the film by the use of the decision Braden had to render concerning the story of the drunken doctor. Incidents concerning this episode appeared in each of the three parts of the film. The conflict was introduced as Braden was seen working in his office at the beginning of the film; it interrupted his family life by calling him away from

home in the middle portion of the picture, and finally this conflict is resolved at the end after a day's work when Braden
directs his colleague to print the story. The students even noticed that a story on the front page of the *Blade-Tribune* as it
came rolling off the press was the story of a local automobile
accident which was seen during a sequence of nocturnal incidents while the narrator reflects that the life of Oceanside goes
on into the night. This same series of shots includes a few plays
from a high school football game. This is the lead story on the
sports page of the next day's paper, seen only for a brief moment as one of the Oceanside residents reads his paper the following evening. Braden's discussion with the city manager
about the need for a new city hall is the topic later used in
dictating his editorial. All these elements of continuity the students had detected as well as more subtle effects used by the
film maker in shifting easily at a change of scene.

The use of symbols was the most important topic on the afternoon agenda. The first and most obvious to the boys were the
shots of the many clocks in the *Blade-Tribune* building. The
students felt this was most effective in creating a mood of tension and urgency as the daily deadline approached. Men and
machines were working a maximum effort to "beat the clock."
They had to overcome the handicap of time in putting out a
daily newspaper. The dumping of the front page plate into the
molten lead was a visual symbol of the narrator's comment
heard simultaneously on the soundtrack: "The making of a
newspaper is a temporary triumph. It must be earned again
each day." The students found many symbols in the one scene
in which Braden stands on the beach at dusk with his son. As
the camera concentrates on a gull winging its way to sea,
Braden speaks: "I'm forty-four. Lots of things in this world I
wanted to do. I'll never get them done now. There's not enough
time. When you're young you don't know that." The boys were
quick to determine the sea gull as a symbol of flight of time,
appropriate to Braden's lament: "There's not enough time."
And some students thought it dramatically and artistically
ironic that he should say this standing before the sea which is

always a symbol of the eternal and timeless. Still others wanted to point out that as Braden said, "When you're young you don't know this," his young son is gleefully skipping rocks into the sea, a symbol of thoughtless youth standing before the imponderables of life.

The picture of the tattoo of the head of Christ crowned with thorns on a man's back was also designated a symbol of the disagreeable element of civic life which a man must work to improve and change if he can. A few thought the shots of Braden walking through the streets of Oceanside by himself at night while determining whether or not to print the story of a drunken doctor subtly figures man's aloneness when confronted with a moral decision. When I asked them to explain the opening frames of the film which pictured a birth, a marriage, and a death, their answers were ready. They were sure that these scenes symbolize the "life" of Oceanside, and since there are no more meaningful events in life than these three, the students considered their choice artistically perfect. Furthermore, these scenes corresponded with an audio symbol on the sound track. The multiple voices of radio newsmen reporting the birth, the marriage, and the death overlap each other so that a seeming confusion is apparent. The boys thought this appropriate because the incidents of "life" which happen in a community do so simultaneously, not separately, and they presumed the film maker imposed many voices at once on the sound track to symbolize this reality. When asked about the parking ticket on Braden's windshield at the end of the picture as he left for home, the students groped a bit before one acute young man said it was the final touch of irony, a symbol of Braden losing this deadline to time.

And time was running out on the afternoon school schedule. I wanted to use the last minutes to question the class on the purpose of our day with this film, and the effectiveness of the teaching. *The Story of a Newspaper Man* we had analyzed closely. That was good. But however important their baptism as film critics, there was something they had learned which was much better. I told them to presume for a moment that there was no NCTE convention in San Francisco, that I was not concerned therefore with giving a report there on our experience with this film, but that I had taught them the film for quite another legitimate and more important reason. What would my reason be? Their answers were appropriate, poignant, and true.

As television-viewers and movie-goers, we are completely passive. As one boy said, we are like the reporters on the *Blade-Tribune* who did not see all the life that was going on around them. We must be like the movie camera and probe into the reality of things. We must pry into movies and films to see what makes them what they are. Added another, "We look but we don't think." We can't talk back to a movie; it's a kind of frustrating monologue, but you want us to somehow answer and make it a dialogue. We are too complacent when viewing films. "No one digs out the theme or purpose, nor does any of us stop to consider a film as a work of art." "You want us to be critical," said one student. "You want us to think," responded another. "You want us to know the truth," replied still one more. And finally one senior said, "You want us to be seekers of truth." So I happily concluded with my own response: "Ah, yes! I want you all to be philosophers."

The Story of a Newspaper Man—Wolper Productions Inc., Hollywood, California

> Series Producer: Mel Stuart
> Written by: Terry Sanders & Robert Fresco
> Produced and directed by: Terry Sanders

Scenes: 1. The Oceanside *Blade-Tribune* lying open on a table;
          2. Thomas W. Braden talking to his staff in his office;
          3. Braden walking through press room.

I—The Newspaper

Sound track:

> 40,000 people depend on the *Blade-Tribune* to give them an honest picture of the world. They depend on

Thomas W. Braden, editor, publisher, owner of the *Blade-Tribune*. For Tom Braden this is the realization of a lifelong dream.

(At this point the title of the film, *The Story of a Newspaper Man*, is imposed on the screen over several still shots:

1. Braden working in his office; 2. Braden standing on the beach with his young son; 3. Braden talking to an aide in the press room.)

Scenes: 1. View of quiet city in early morning;
2. Closeup of newly born infant yawning;
3. A bride dressing for her wedding;
4. Sad crowd witnessing funeral services at a cemetery.

Sound track:

Radio reporters chronicling news of the past day and night: the temperature, time, birth announcements, marriage rites, death and funeral notices. Gradually many voices overlap each other on the sound track with the multiple and varied news concerning the population of Oceanside, California.

Scenes: 1. John Wilkins, the narrator, in front of a huge newspaper stand introducing himself and the theme of the film;
2. Supermarket shoppers in Oceanside being interviewed for opinion of Thomas W. Braden and the *Blade-Tribune*.

Sound track:

Who, what, when, where, why, how: the newspaper is a powerful voice. It informs, persuades, entertains. In Oceanside, California, the newspaper is one man: Thomas W. Braden, editor and publisher. In the words of William Allen White, the most famous small town newspaper man of them all: "There are three things no man can do to any other man's satisfaction: make love, poke the fire, and run a newspaper." At this point several contrary opinions of Thomas W. Braden and his newspaper are given by those interviewed and the final remark is by an elderly woman: "We think he's fearless and fair."

II—Thomas W. Braden, The Man

Scenes: 1. Braden almost tardy for flight on American Airlines;
2. Braden golfing with Pat Brown, governor of California;
3. Braden presiding at a meeting of the California Board of Education.

Sound track:

Two months of the year Thomas Braden is on the move from Washington, D.C., to Russia trying to find out what's going on in the world, what people are thinking. His continuing interest in education led Governor Brown to appoint him president of the California Board of Education.

Scenes: 1. Exterior of the *Blade-Tribune* building in Oceanside;
2. On the inside, shots of awards, emblems, and trophies won by the *Blade-Tribune* since Braden's ownership;
3. Presses running;
4. Braden watching, walking, reflecting about his newspaper;
5. Braden studying a copy of the *Blade-Tribune*.

Sound track:

The rest of the year Thomas Braden spends in Oceanside, California, in this building, the home of the

Blade-Tribune. Braden's voice: "You carry around an image of what you think the newspaper should look like. Sometimes you succeed and sometimes you don't." There never seems to be enough time to make the printed page conform to the mental image.

Scenes: 1. Braden walking upstairs to his office still studying the paper;
2. Braden chewing out his staff for improper writing and reporting;
3. Closeups of the youthful staff members as Braden minces no words.

Sound track:

Braden's voice: It is difficult to maintain quality in a newspaper. Writers get careless and articles become sterile. Braden directs his remarks to spelling, grammar, and leads and compares the *Blade-Tribune* to a high school sheet and reading like a notice column. "The newspaper should reflect what the town is." Sometimes a reporter's eyes become closed. "There's a whole lot of life around."

Scenes: 1. Firemen working to control a blaze;
2. Reporter talking to woman holding a child, owner of the burning house;
3. Beauty contest winner posing in bathing suit;
4. Joyful people showering rice on recently married couple;
5. Dredging barge at work in the bay;
6. Small boy kneeling next to a tall, prize turkey;
7. Note: in each of these scenes a reporter is present with his pencil and notebook diligently plying his trade.

Sound track:

The newspaper is a "mirror of everything" that happens in a small town. "The newspaper must capture the total community."

Scenes: 1. Braden working in his office;
         2. Braden conversing with staff member concerning a news story.

Sound track:

"People's troubles" become a part of Braden's work as a newspaper man. "Deciding to print the tough truth" is one of the difficulties of his job. Braden must decide whether to print the story of a doctor arrested for drunk driving or not.

Scenes: 1. Braden driving through Oceanside;
         2. Exterior of clothing store;
         3. Inside, conversations with story owner about advertising;
         4. Exterior and sign of used car lot;
         5. Closeups of Braden bargaining with car salesman about more advertising.

Sound track:

Eighty-five percent of the *Blade-Tribune's* income comes from advertising and not from subscribers. Braden attempts to persuade the clothier of the ineffectiveness of direct, "junk" mail advertising and vainly tries to sell more advertising space to the car dealer.

Scenes: 1. Braden arriving at home in his car;
         2. Front view of his twelve-room house on the beach;
         3. Little daughter coming down a slide and landing in the sand;
         4. Same little girl romping off to the beach;
         5. Members of the Braden family playing touch-football on the beach;

6. Family skipping along the beach at dusk;
7. Braden standing with his son looking out to the ocean;
8. A gull winging its way out to sea.

Sound track:

Thomas Braden lives with his family in this twelve-room house situated near the beach in Oceanside, California. Braden's voice: He introduces his family as they play on the beach. While commenting on their desire to have a large family, he mentions each of the children. There are seven. Then says Braden: "I'm forty-four. Lots of things in this world I wanted to do. I'll never get them done now. There's not enough time. When you're young, you don't know that."

Scenes: 1. Braden family in their living room;
2. Tom Braden reading the *Blade-Tribune;*
3. Children reading books and playing games;
4. The baby insisting on its rightful place, Mrs. Braden's lap.

Sound track:

The realistic clatter of children's conversation accompanied with the oral reading exercises of one of his little daughters while the baby is squalling for his mother's attention.

Scenes: 1. From inside the Braden house to a night view of Oceanside;
2. An automobile accident involving injury to several;
3. A local high school football game and the omnipresent reporter;
4. Back to the exterior of the Braden house at night.

Sound track:

The wail of a siren interrupts the silence of the eve-

ning as the narrator remarks that the "life of Oceanside goes on into the night." The incidents and activities of night provide the reading matter for tomorrow's
newspaper. The night silence is again shattered, this
time by a telephone call to Mr. Braden.

Scenes: 1. Braden answering phone;
        2. Braden meeting stranger at Marty's Restaurant;
        3. Stranger in topcoat and tilted hat only seen from
           the back talking to Braden at a booth in the restau-
           rant.

Sound track:

The episode of the drunk doctor is reintroduced at this
nocturnal meeting in an attempt to persuade Braden
not to print the story. Braden remarks that he
wouldn't think of not printing the story when he first
came to Oceanside. "I'm more reasonable now." He
worries about the doctor's children reading about it in
the newspaper. Braden still remains undecided about
printing the story as he ruminates: "This man might
have killed somebody."

Scenes: 1. Braden walking through the business district of the
           city at night;
        2. Exterior of a tattoo shop called The Arcade;
        3. Close-up of a tattoo of the head of Christ crowned
           with thorns on a man's back;
        4. Braden stopping, looking at this tattoo, and think-
           ing to himself;
        5. Braden walking away smoking, thinking.

Sound track:

Braden's voice: "I wish I could think a newspaper
publisher has no more power than anyone else. But he
does. He does if he has a sense of responsibility about
his town. I might not like a lot of things about Ocean-

side, so I'll criticize it. But it's my town. My roots are
here. Roots are important to me. I can go anywhere
in the world and say: 'My name is Braden, I'm from
Oceanside, and I run the newspaper there.' "

III—Thomas W. Braden, The Newspaper Man

Scenes: 1. Braden driving away from home to work in the
   morning;
2. Braden with secretary in his office scheduling social
   civic and private functions;
3. Braden driving around Oceanside with the City
   Manager, Frank Lilly;
4. Junk yards, rundown dwellings, littered property
   that are found along entrance route to Oceanside;
5. Braden and Lilly discussing city problems while
   standing on one of the city's bridges.

Sound track:

Braden tells his secretary he will accept invitations to
the Tri-City Board of Directors Meeting and Dr. Simp-
son's retirement party. He and Frank Lilly talk of the
growing city, its future, its need for a cleanup program
and its need for a new city hall. Lilly wants to know
if Braden will support these civic projects in his newspaper.

Scenes: 1. Braden returning to his *Blade-Tribune* office;
2. Whole sequence of scenes dealing with the production of a newspaper; reporters typing up stories,
   linotype machines in operation, teletypes ticking off
   news, page planners, proofreading, Braden dictating
   his editorial, wire service machines, making of printing plates, readying of the presses and so on;
3. Frequent shots of different clocks beginning at
   11: 00 a.m. until the presses roll at 2: 30 p.m.;
4. Shots of many employees diligently pursuing their
   tasks;

5. The presses rolling out a newspaper—drums, cylinders, and paper whirling together with frightful speed.

Sound track:

"A newspaper is ruled by its deadline." Stories must be written by 11:45. (The noises of all the machines from typewriters to presses is heard on the sound track.) Braden and his colleagues must choose lead story from the many wire services. Braden dictates his editorial about the need for a new city hall for a city of 30,000 people. The unruly noises of the pressroom dominate this section of the film until finally the presses are started and the newsprint screams through the press with its peculiar whine.

Scenes: 1. Braden reading newest edition of the *Blade-Tribune* in his office;
2. Copies of the paper rapidly flopping off the press;
3. Newsboy on bicycle delivering the paper to homes;
4. An Oceanside resident reading the *Blade-Tribune* sports section in his living room.

Sound track:

Noise of the presses is contrasted to the quiet of the city street at dusk. The narrator quotes Thomas Jefferson: "Were it left to me to decide whether we should have government without a newspaper or a newspaper without government I should not hesitate a moment to prefer the latter."

Scenes: 1. Broker trying to persuade Braden to sell the *Blade-Tribune;*
2. Close-ups of both men during this dialogue.

Sound track:

The conversation between Braden and the newspaper

broker. Braden is told his newspaper is worth one million dollars. He replies that he considers buying and selling a newspaper immoral. Says Braden: "I can't imagine not being a newspaper man." "What makes me most happy is running the *Blade-Tribune*."

Scenes: 1. A view of the city at night;
2. Braden in his office working;
3. As he leaves his office, Braden stops and directs his aide to print the story of the drunk doctor;
4. Cleanup boy dumps front page plate into molten lead;
5. This metal plate melting in the hot lead;
6. Cleanup boy picking up all loose newspapers from the floor;
7. Shots of all machines still and quiet;
8. Braden removing parking ticket from windshield of his car before driving home after a day's work.

Sound track:

Braden's voice: "Hey, Jerry! You know that story about the doctor? Well, print it!" Narrator's voice: "The making of a newspaper is a temporary triumph. It must be earned again each day." In a newspaper "What you really see is what life is, what America is."

Credits

The End

LITERATURE AND THE MASS MEDIA

Eric Ivary

English 12-1

The movie *The Story of a Newspaper Man* confronted me with a novel dilemma. The class first glanced passively at a motion picture; then the same class systematically dismantled it.

Upon this closer analysis, I came upon an entirely new concept that I have never seen or looked for in a film. My eyes had been thoroughly glossed over by the sloppy superficial methods of present mass media, television in particular. But this one twenty-seven minute production grasped in its short reach an enormous concept, with applications to television, radio, and all newspapers. The documentary about a man and his own expression of art contains elements ordinarily expected only in artistic forms, or more exactly, in conventional artistic forms. However, this film is art.

In the film there is a literary continuity that usually goes unnoticed in cinema but is nevertheless evidenced in this one. There are beautifully coordinated binding factors in this brief film. The clock on the way in the reporters' room; the continually humming machines gather in the news, shape it, and mould it into a newspaper. There is never an abrupt shift of scenes; the camera wanders not as it pleases but as it is intended. The camera lingers in Braden's office with his eyes, with his thoughts, always coinciding with the narration. The camera focuses on the newspaper at the start, then on to its creator, then to a jumble of life in Oceanside as it is similarly muddled by the verbal commentary of many voices. Another binding element is the problem of the doctor. A doctor who was arrested for drunk driving wants his name kept out of the paper. The decision is up to Braden only, but this situation involves his ever growing realization that he cannot tamper with the truth. This question arises at the beginning, middle, and end of the film where it is finally resolved and the story is printed.

As literature, this movie also has a harmony, a selectivity of the mass of facts and incidents, important occurrences and trivial matters. Daily there is a torrent of life rushing into the newspaper office, and it is Braden's job to select what words will appear in his paper to represent what has happened in the life of Oceanside and the world. The paper is designed to be a substitute for experience. In the film a fire and a football game occur once in reality and once in print. The movie itself embraces the same harmony as the newspaper described in it. The

film has twenty-seven minutes to accomplish its purpose. It
does so admirably. What a fund of details there must be in an
editor's routine, yet in twenty-seven minutes we saw his whole
day with the newspaper. The producers of this movie selected
only representative and significant incidents in his day, giving
emphasis to each in proportion to its value. The office, the
presses, the daily tasks, such as placating a used car dealer
complaining about advertising, the home, all these form a mini-
ature cross-section of Tom Braden's life. There is an order in
this movie as there is in life.

The third property this movie possesses in common with art
is radiance, that is, a penetration into man as a person. Unlike
the ordinary movie, *The Story of a Newspaper Man* lapses into
profundity and philosophical dilemmas which I previously not
only had never looked for but never dreamed existed in a
medium such as a film. Because of the close analysis of our
class, this film was found to be rich with philosophical ideas
from Tom Braden. There are two examples of this. In the scene
showing Braden on the beach with his son, looking wistfully
out to sea, he comments on an old problem: his own youthful
ambition has found its fulfillment far short of its originally anticipated goal. He realizes that time is a pressing reality, always
harping, always pushing until Tom Braden (and every man) is
jostled into the grim confines of minutes and hours. During
this same scene his young son is throwing rocks into the ocean
as if to hit some distant shore. Another important concept
streams from the film in a scene at the room containing the
huge presses. Here there is another of man's frustrations ex-
emplified by one of Tom Braden's. The printing plates, the locus
of attention and activity for a whole day, after that day are
useless. They are heaved into the melting pot to become incor-
porated into tomorrow and tomorrow. So it is with many of
man's worldly treasures; they are dust and are daily returned
to dust.

This film is art in the same sense as books, paintings, or
music. Within the movie itself, Braden demonstrated that a
newspaper can incorporate the qualities of art—unity, har-

mony, and radiance—even in its limited scope. But there is nothing impeding television, radio, and other mass media from assuming the same qualities. Instead of bogging down the already intellectually crushed television viewers, television could effect changes which would stimulate the mind rather than insult it. For example, television shows might reapportion commercials and make use of visual literary devices; and these changes could make this unruly king of the mass media the most absorbing form of art in history.

AN EDUCATIONAL EXPERIMENT

Bob San Souci

English 12-1

The presentation of the movie on Thomas Braden—*The Story of a Newspaper Man*—and the subsequent discussions on the documentary gradually centered on two main areas: first, the potential of the cinema as an art form on a comparative level with literature; second, an investigation of the concepts underlying the material presented. The latter would include reasons for making the picture (the concern of the creators) and the effect of this picture on the viewer—the stimulation of thought and new ideas.

The first section discussed was the cinema as an aesthetic development. Motion pictures have undergone a metamorphosis since the days of the Mack Sennett Keystone Cops. Today there are many so-called "art" films that have been cast ashore as the flotsam from the "New Wave," the common term used to describe the trend in film making toward highly stylistic and frequently off-beat productions. The viewer is forced to decide whether this is "art" for the sake of effect—more novelty, shock, and so forth; or if it is "ars gratia artis." Our discussion of the film presented some basic criteria for evaluating a picture, since it was itself a legitimate attempt to create beauty through the medium of the camera.

For the most part the film was composed of various episodes in the life of a newspaperman—episodes that, like a mosaic, served to form a structural whole. In lucid manner the film chronicled his actions, giving them continuity by concentrating on two days in the man's life. There was a plot of sorts (or sub-plot, as the publication of the newspaper may be considered the central interest of the film): the question of whether or not to publish the story of an intoxicated doctor. Three brief sequences served to bring the problem into focus, to delineate the various aspects of it, and finally to resolve it. This added a hint of suspense to the proceedings and served to cement the various portions of the film more firmly. Symbolism also played a major role in the film; such visual imagery as melting down the molds of yesterday's newspaper to convey the idea of the newspaper's preoccupation with the present. Just as the writer makes use of figures of speech to embellish his work, so did the photographer use the tricks of his trade to heighten the effect of the picture on the viewer. The camera paused to ponder an evening on the seashore, and there was almost tangible poignancy in the scene; the camera rushed along, following the newspapers as they were hurried through to publication, and the onlooker was caught up in the breakneck tempo of the printing world. Even the musical score, with its pulsating rhythm, complemented the visual dramatics.

The criteria, then, for an artful picture are continuity, clearly defined theme or focal point, the use of visual effects (within reason), and such peripheral additions as scoring. This is not to suggest that a film which seemingly lacks any form of continuity or one devoid of a musical score cannot be an artful picture. The former may convey some mood or abstract concept by its very formlessness, while the lack of music in the latter may serve to heighten dramatic impact. Basically, the determination of a picture's artfulness comes from the film maker's ability to blend the elements of the film together into a pleasing presentation. Two films may be as different as the *Mona Lisa* and the current "pop art" with its enlarged comic strips. The viewer must decide whether or not a picture is artful. Art is

beauty; and ultimately, "Beauty is in the eye of the beholder."
The picture, *The Story of a Newspaper Man*, together with the
dissection and discussion of it, serves to make that eye more
perceptive, more responsive, perhaps more particular when
seeking to discern what is or is not art.

The second major point under consideration was the use of
the movie as a format for presenting complex and abstract concepts to the viewer for consideration. In "Thomas B." there was
a question of morality regarding the story of the drunken
doctor: Should the newspaper preserve the doctor's reputation
in deference to "doctor-patient relationships," or should he
accede to his sense of responsibility in regard to a potentially
unfit doctor? The protagonist decides one way; by the time the
facts are known, the viewer may well have felt that a different
decision was preferable. The emphasis in the picture was not
so much telling the reader what the answer should be, but primarily to get him to ponder the question. In literature a striking
concept will have a mental—or, at best, an audio-mental impact
upon the reader. The same person, when viewing a picture such
as this one and its concept of newspaper morality, will receive
an audiovisual-mental impact. The viewer should be aware of
and responsive to the stimuli to thought apparent in a well-
constructed picture.

What applies here to movies applies to television, but to a
lesser degree. Television, since it has found the various formulas (situation comedies, westerns, soap operas) for mass
appeal, is less open to experimentation than the motion picture,
which seeks to draw the people back to theaters on the basis
of innovation. There have been on occasion various TV programs of real substance ("Greece: The Golden Age"), but such
appearances are sporadic, and television seems destined to confine itself mainly to frivolity.

The discussion on mass media and literature was continued
and expanded in San Francisco. The session was extremely
informative. Our group stated the conclusions we had already
come to, and when questioned on various aspects of the field as
yet untouched, we stated our various opinions in these cases

also. The discussion centered on the handicaps and poten-
tials of television programing as art, then shifted to such diverse
topics as newspaper journalism and its relation to literature.
Even when the actual queries had ceased, we held forth in the
halls on various related ideas. One interesting topic was the
question of adapting works of literature to the screen. Do the
original pieces suffer in the translation? The conclusion (more
correctly, the opinion) was that it depends upon the translator
or scenario writer. *To Kill a Mockingbird* came across as an
effective and powerful piece of cinematography, with the substance of the novel kept intact; while the bulk of *Moby Dick*
was discarded in preference to a fifty-foot model of the white
whale and an exact replica of the Pequod. This serves as a
random sampling to indicate the scope and depth of the discussions, which I hope were as informative to the coordinators as
to us.

In short, the educational experiment brought to the fore several prerequisites for studying mass media:

1. To be familiar with the basic structure of the documentary, television show, newspaper article, etc., and to be able
to appreciate the elements that compose the piece.

2. To look for some underlying concept behind the making
of the picture: social criticism, the presentation of a question
of morality, or whatever.

3. AND, if the artist has unsuccessfully developed the first
two ideas—*not* to become so enraptured with examination
of the parts that the effectiveness of the whole is lost.

LESSON PLAN FOR *The Story of a Newspaper Man*

I. The film content

    A. As a profile of a small town publisher

        1. Thomas Braden is revealed as possessing certain char-
           acter traits that probably would have made him a
           success regardless of his choice of a career.

Cite sequences in the film that illustrate his character:

  a. His relationship with his family, his employees, his fellow townspeople;

  b. His pride in his daily product, the *Blade-Tribune* newspaper;

  c. His concern for his community;

  d. His objectivity;

  e. His integrity;

  f. His acceptance of responsibility.

2. Having these admirable traits, Mr. Braden is able to give the scope by knowing his job. Cite instances in the film of that knowledge:

  a. His periodic staff meetings;

  b. His "tours" of the plant;

  c. His world travel;

  d. His "extracurricular" reading at home;

  e. His conferences with the city manager;

  f. His attendance at civic and private functions;

  g. His recommendations for civic improvements;

  h. His constructive editorial policy.

B. As an analysis of the function of a newspaper

1. The film stresses Mr. Braden's philosophy:

  a. To show what the town is;

  b. To work for civic improvement;

  c. Human interest vs. "notices" from a police blotter;

  d. An editorial policy based on the publisher-editor's roots in the community.

2. The film suggests certain significant questions pertaining to newspapers generally:

  a. Hometown ownership vs. absentee or syndicate control;

  b. Advertiser's influence on editorial policy;

  c. Civic leadership vs. carping criticism;

  d. Freedom of the press limited with the responsibility of the press.

II. The film as film

    A. A cinematic technique unique to film (or TV) is used to introduce *The Story of a Newspaper Man*. Comment on the effectiveness of the flashes of small town events, such as the wedding, the funeral, the fire, each with its overlapping commentary, to absorb the viewer.

    B. The film communicates on many levels of meaning. Among other things, discuss:

       1. The symbolism of the melting of the day's plates after the press run;

       2. The juxtaposition of the newly born baby in the hospital with the funeral cortege at the cemetery;

       3. The irony of the head of Christ as a tattoo;

       4. The irony of Braden finding a parking ticket on his car at the finale.

    C. Cite instances of effective photography direction:

       1. The silhouette scenes of Braden's children on the beach;

       2. The closeups of his little girl as she finishes her reading lesson and looks proudly at her father;

       3. The aloneness of the publisher as he walks the deserted street at night and makes his decision in the case of the drunken doctor.